Drawing on years of pastoral care and chaplaincy experience, *Habits of Resilience* offers concrete strategies for building the spiritual resilience we all need in times of bereavement. Beryl Schewe's vivid storytelling will get your attention, and her practical wisdom will earn your trust.

❊ **Dan McKanan**, Harvard Divinity School

This excellent and accessible resource is both a practical guide that examines all kinds of grief and a deeply spiritual one for times in our lives that require alternating and simultaneous measures of both.

❊ **Bishop Sally Dyck**, Episcopal leader of the Northern Illinois Annual Conference of The United Methodist Church

---

Beryl Schewe has given us much more than a how-to book. Her guide shows us the skills we need to work through our inevitable grief, and it teaches us how to develop them. But be prepared to weep a bit. Her stories will touch your heart—and lead us all to become more resilient! I have already recommended it to a friend.

❊ **Irene Nowell, OSB**, author of *Pleading, Cursing, Praising: Conversing with God through the Psalms*

Beryl Schewe is a wise and compassionate guide on life's journey. She writes with grace and respect from her own experience as one who has given practical spiritual care for many years.

❊ **Zara Renander**, author of *Labyrinths: Journeys of Healing Stories of Grace*

No one needs to be mired in grief. In *Habits of Resilience,* Beryl Schewe shows us how to be intentional and active participants in our own inevitable grief journeys. She also tells us how to offer compassionate and practical guidance to other persons dealing with loss and grief. Drawing from personal experiences as well as her many years in pastoral care ministry, she presents a book that looks upon experiences of grief as rich and positive opportunities for growth, and for loving, healing service to others. Her use of stories and case studies makes this a moving and engaging read for any Christian seeking to make sense out of loss and unexpected life changes. This is an especially helpful resource for anyone engaged in church ministry.

✳ **BERNARD EVANS, PHD.**, ASSOCIATE DEAN,
   ST JOHN'S SCHOOL OF THEOLOGY

This is a compelling, authentic, beautifully crafted book that shines with wisdom, grace, and experience. Grief can be a lonely place, but Beryl Schewe shows it doesn't have to be. Read it, weep, learn, and wonder. Schewe's lifetime spent providing pastoral care to the grieving can't have been easy; her wisdom has been hard-won. All of us can now benefit from it in terms of how we live, how we face up to our own mortality, how we grieve, and how we support those we love in their grief. From now on, I hope that when I think of grief, I will think too of the quiet marvel that is resilience.

✳ **JUDITH O'REILLY,** FORMER BBC JOURNALIST AND AUTHOR
   OF THE BESTSELLING BOOK *Wife in the North*

HABITS *of* RESILIENCE

LEARNING TO LIVE FULLY
IN THE MIDST OF LOSS

A grief workbook with

practices and reflections

for healing and growth

BERYL SCHEWE

TWENTY
THIRD 23rd
PUBLICATIONS
www.23rdpublications.com

To Steve,

Thomas, Sarah,

& Wynona Jane

SECOND PRINTING

Twenty-Third Publications

1 Montauk Avenue, Suite 200, New London, CT 06320

(860) 437-3012 » (800) 321-0411 » www.23rdpublications.com

ISBN: 978-1-62785-105-3

Library of Congress Catalog Card Number: 2015939729

Printed in the U.S.A.

Contents

Speaking to grief

Moving through grief to grace

Prologue

"Life is changed, not ended."

When lives change—by death; by grief—the world seems to stop. Death holds up a mirror and brings hard questions about the mystery of existence to the surface of our lives. If life does not end with death, what does end? Where does whatever is left of us go after we die? How do we as survivors carry on after the death of a loved one, a friend, or a colleague? What do life and death mean to us? We barely have language for questions so large. Our answers never fully capture the mystery of faith.

Consider the communion of saints. Many of us speak to those beyond the grave, praying to and with our loved ones. Our relationship with them still exists, even as it defies explanation and invites the scoffing of skeptics. I don't pretend to understand this, or to speak for God. All I can do is faithfully recount the stories I've heard of life, death, faith, and resilience amidst the dying and the bereaved. I do know that these stories tell about the best we can offer to ourselves and others. For those who are dying or mourning a death, there is often no room for anything else. My work with the bereaved offers me a rare privilege—to stand with and hear the stories of families at their most authentic and defining moments.

How do we move on, allowing the deep losses in our lives to become part of our story but not our whole story? The stories are everyday examples of recovery and resilience, ordinary people who understand the searing pain of the biblical expression to "gnash your teeth." All of us want more than simply surviving grief. Stories show us the paths back to living full and resilient lives in a world of loss. That is our challenge.

In time, many do make meaning from their losses. Their stories shine a light onto the pathways of the resilience that they discover. We won't walk the same road. Our journey through grief will be ours alone. Perhaps knowing others have wrestled down grief's unquench-able fears will give us hope. We might even try on some of the habits of resilience to see what fits. Some who shared their stories with me requested I use their actual names; other stories are composites of a number of people and events. To preserve the anonymity of these indi-viduals and their families, I've changed significant details and blended stories together. Several of the stories were originally published in the *Eden Prairie News*, my local paper where I am a columnist.

Jesus, the great healer, asked, "Do you want to be healed?" Jesus recognized that *we have to choose a healing path*, not simply hope and assume that time will heal all wounds.

For those who would prefer a non-religious analogy, let me add: How many psychiatrists does it take to change a light bulb? Only one, but the light bulb has to want to change. We need to be active participants in our grief journey.

Zara Renander, author and founder of Turning Point Consultants, works with veterans, helping them move towards reconciliation. To help veterans move through their grief, Renander pays particular attention to resilience. Merriam-Webster defines resilience simply: the ability to become strong, healthy, or successful again after something bad happens or the ability of something to return to its original shape after it has been pulled, stretched, pressed, bent, etc. For Renander, the goal of resilience after loss is not returning to our "original shape," but integrating our past and present so we might move forward.

> The word "resilient" may conjure up the image of a rubber band which after it's stretched has physical memory and springs back into its original shape. The resilient spirit, however, is one that has the flexibility to endure the stretching of the original, comfortable shape, and then has the ability to transcend that shape moving into a new dimension of ourselves. Human beings need to make meaning of their lives, and resiliency skills help us to reconcile the past and present, allowing us to move into a healthy future. It is a work that takes a lifetime of practice.[1]

Resilience is the capacity to bounce back from life's traumas and to thrive in adverse circumstances. Our focus shifts from what has happened to us to how we respond to those experiences.

Resilience is the subject of great debate and research these days.

---

1   Zara Renander, Turning Point Consultants Spiritual Resiliency training at Fort Benning, GA US Army Post, 2014. www.TurningPointConsultants.com.

Why do some people seem naturally more resilient than others? Are they born with a genetic predisposition towards resilience? Regardless of our disposition, resilience is a skill that can be developed.

Resilience can be strengthened and cultivated in our life. We have the capacity to become more resilient, develop stronger and more loving relationships, and live fuller lives. Cultivating resilience, I believe, begins with gratitude.

I'd like to tell you I wrote this book for you, so you might traverse the minefields of grief with greater agility and resilience. But I did not. I wrote this book for me. It is a view from my window, and a remembrance of some of the lovely people who have touched my life and gone before me to show me the way. How do we live as people of faith, knowing we will die? That, it seems, is the ultimate question each of us must answer. Does love triumph over death?

Finding our resilient roots

I'm not sure when I first knew that I was going to die. Looking back, my early life lessons established a strong family preference for avoidance. If something was painful or produced fear and anxiety, we didn't discuss it. This covered a lot of territory, including death.

When I was nine, my sister and I spent the better part of a summer in California with my paternal grandparents, W.C. and Rosa. When my sister and I returned home to Connecticut, we discovered the real reason for the summer "grandparent camp" in California. My parents had moved across town to a rental house as they built our new home.

How I had not taken in the reality of the move is beyond me. Years before, my parents had bought land where they were now building, and we'd spent nearly every available weekend that spring helping my dad site the house. And by siting the house, I mean running a string line to mimic the perimeter of the house. Standing on one side of the string, we would look out of imaginary windows to take in the view. The string was moved, angled, and tweaked until my dad felt he had optimized the view of our backyard.

You'd think all those hours looking out imaginary windows would have clued me in to the timing of our new house. But I was nine, and delighted to have adults standing behind a piece of string with me imagining we were all looking out a window. The view was not as rosy when I returned from California. I had a tiny blue bedroom in a rental house across town, away from my friends, my school, and my familiar bike routes.

School started, and my older sister headed to the junior high, a school that blended all the elementary schools—her friends would be there. I headed to a new and different elementary school, where there were no friends and no familiar faces.

Just weeks into school, one of my sister's classmates, Trudy, was thrown from a horse in a horse show. The bridle was loose, and everyone in the ring could see it. Apparently the crowd shouted for Trudy to jump off her horse, but the meaning of a crowd screaming "jump" in a horse show designed for horses to jump was lost in translation. Trudy stayed on the horse, the horse made the jump, and Trudy was thrown off.

Trudy was knocked unconscious. The crowd called for emergency services, but Trudy's parents were Christian Scientists. They bundled her up, took her home, and presumably prayed that Trudy would be healed. A few days later, Trudy died of her head injury.

Other than baby birds found at the base of a tree and crabs surreptitiously brought home from the beach, this was my first experience of death. My grandmother, also a Christian Scientist, spent the last forty years of her life trying to convince me to join her faith. What she didn't know was that by ten, I'd already ruled it out. Christian Scientists died.

The following summer, my granddad died of a massive heart attack. Granddad had "indigestion" for years but never really explored the possibility of heart disease. I suspect his failure to get better medical care was directly related to my grandmother's Christian Science faith. My grandmother, who lived without the benefit of doctors, medicine, alcohol, or caffeine, lived to 103. Go figure.

I took all this in, and the promise of resilience I made to myself was to simply not die by avoiding horses and my grandmother's church. So far, this has worked.

By my twenties, I had a more expansive understanding of death: all people die. Of course, by "all people" I meant older people—not me, my friends, or my parents. This definition held up until a college classmate collapsed on the campus quadrangle at an art fair. The North Carolina sun was especially warm that day, and oddly, the young woman was wearing a waterproof track suit designed to make a person sweat profusely. Everyone thought she'd passed out. But she hadn't; her heart had stopped. She was anorexic; it appeared she had worn the waterproof track suit as part of her continuing efforts to lose even more weight. This story had a tragic ending.

Her death right there on the quad did not alter my understanding of death. As much as I comprehended the realities of death, I had managed to cordon it off to a couple of distinct and avoidable categories: children of Christian Scientists who ride horses with loose bridles or people who struggle with anorexia. I was pretty sure the rest of us were safe.

My thirties and forties presented more opportunities to chip away at my defenses around death. My grandmothers and my husband's grandmothers all died, which left me one generation closer to death, but comfortably behind all four living parents.

Then 9/11 happened. I grew up in Connecticut in one of New York City's bedroom communities. My dad commuted to New York City for most of my life, and the commuter railroad schedule was part of the cadence of our day. We ate dinner when Dad got home. If he missed the train, which happened infrequently, we ate an hour later.

The train became an odd and unlikely locus of grief on 9/11. Phone service on the East Coast was almost non-existent in the days immediately following the attack, so my parents' neighbors went door to door, accounting for all of the neighbors. Had they all come home? Where did they work? By midday, the neighbors had some sense of who was still unaccounted for. And so the vigil began.

Without phones, my parents' small town relied on a more primitive transfer of information. They went down to the train station and waited. Train by train arrived from New York City and as people disembarked, families hugged and wept grateful tears of relief. As each train arrived, the crowd thinned, and the anxiety rose. Then the last train arrived. This is how my parents' next-door neighbor discovered that her husband would never come home again. He wasn't on the last train.

After 9/11, there was a brief uptick in the practice of going to church, people either reconnecting with the sacred in their lives or asking God exactly what the hell was going on. Or both. We felt vulnerable. We knew death was random, and we knew that some day we too might not be on that last train.

By my fifties, my parents died and my father-in-law had died. I was a chaplain by then, and my day-to-day work life involved working with the dying.

If our history informs our future responses, then surely my history with death is what shook me to the ground when my friend Lisa died. Lisa had done everything right. She had on a bike helmet and she was riding on a bike trail. Like my parents' neighbor who didn't make the last train, Lisa was simply in the wrong place at the wrong time. The city has since added safety features to the bike tunnel where Lisa collided with another cyclist, but Lisa is still gone, and I miss her.

Unlike my nine-year-old world where I could change the view from my imaginary window by adjusting the string line of my imaginary house, the harsh view of Lisa's death was full frame.

Habit of resilience

PRACTICE THE "CASE METHOD"

Many business schools employ the Case Method of learning. Instead of teaching theoretical models, students study actual situations, discerning how they might introduce positive change within given circumstances. Sixty students would suggest sixty different scenarios to move forward. This is what I invite you to do—look through the lens of another's grief journey and ponder ways you might move forward if you were in their shoes.

The Case Method is also often affectionately referred to as "Copy And Steal Everything," a mantra that refers to businesses incorporating best practices gleaned from other companies. In the same manner, I invite you to try on the habits of resilience you notice in these stories and in your everyday life.

REFLECTION

It is unlikely most of us would have named our early experiences of death or loss as "grief." Yet even as children, we developed coping strategies to weather our difficult times. Can you remember ways you were resilient or ways that you coped amidst the grief and loss in your childhood?

How has your view of death changed since you were a child? How have your coping strategies changed? Can you name ways you have developed greater resilience in your life?

Saying our goodbyes

❈ 1 ❈

RESILIENCE AT
THE TIME OF DEATH

When I was eleven, the unthinkable happened. My Uncle Dwight and six-year-old cousin Scotty went on the trip of a lifetime, a father/son fishing trip, just five dads, five young boys, and a pilot in a private plane. My uncle's plane was missing for a week before search and rescue discovered the crash site. Experts believe the plane got caught in a freak late-spring snowstorm and crashed into a canyon wall. Everyone on the plane was killed. There were no remains. My aunt was handed a palm-sized piece of deformed and melted metal: her husband's watch.

My Aunt Marianne and her two other children began the long process of grieving a husband and son, a father and brother.

A few years later, my Aunt Marianne remarried when my cousins were teens. Not long after, her husband, Don, was diagnosed with ALS, Lou Gehrig's disease. It was a long, painful goodbye, and it seemed terribly unfair that once again my aunt was burying another husband.

I asked her once which was the harder goodbye. "Dwight's," she said without blinking. "I never got to say goodbye."

Years ago, when I worked as a hospital chaplain, I was paged to see a patient in the middle of an icy night. As treacherous as was my journey through an ice storm, his journey was a thousand times more precarious.

When I arrived, Jack's wife and a cousin were sitting in the ICU's waiting area. The nurse introduced us, and Jack's cousin filled the air with small talk and then asked, "Do you always work the third shift?" It hit me full force; they didn't know. They thought I'd just happened by and this was a random encounter with a third-shift chaplain. The family did not know that I had been paged specifically for them, that thirty minutes before I'd been sound asleep in a cloud of down comforters. They did not know that Jack was not expected to see morning's light and that this very night they would be praying their goodbyes.

Jack had been diagnosed with an aggressive cancer and had thrown himself into a demanding treatment plan. He was married and had two school-age girls, three good reasons to endure a grueling chemo regimen. He'd been given a likely survival time of two years. That was ten months ago. These dates would prove to be an impediment for Jack's wife. She and Jack had already survived several middle-of-the-night ICU hospital admissions, and she believed tonight was just another scare. She fully expected fourteen more months, and as the night progressed and Jack's situation became grave, she continued to say, "We just have to pull him through."

She did not know she would be the one who would need to pull through. She would be the one to help Jack cross from life to death. She would be the one to bravely coach her girls through this unexpected, unwanted journey, this painful goodbye that would sear their hearts.

Sometimes we don't know things we should. Sometimes we are surrounded by signs as big as billboards that we fail to notice. When we finally get it, we wonder how we could possibly have missed the obvious signals. Jack's nurse came out and knelt down on one knee so she was eye to eye with his wife. Quietly and seriously, she said, "Your husband is very, very sick." Jack's wife said again, "We just have to pull him through." This had become her mantra, as if words could provide a protective shield for what was about to happen, what will happen to us all.

Quite suddenly, she understood. I had been both dreading this moment and actively encouraging the medical team to be more forthright, so that Jack's wife might come to an awareness of her husband's impending death before someone emerged from the hallway mouthing the dreaded words, "I am so sorry." Jack was actively dying; she knew this now.

A heartbeat before, she was enduring yet another long night in her husband's cancer treatment. Now her life was about to change forever. It was time to gather her girls and to pray their goodbyes for a husband and father who would never again in this life be able to say he loved her, never again to squeeze her hand, never to stay up with her waiting for a beloved grandchild to be born.

Sometimes grace arrives and fills us so completely that we are able to do things beyond our imagining. I'd encouraged Jack's wife and daughters to each spend time with Jack and tell him they loved him. Even though he wasn't conscious, they could ask his forgiveness, forgive him for any lingering resentments, and let him know that they would miss him but that they would be okay. When he was ready to go to God, he could go. I reminded them that hearing was the last sense to go before death and that even though Jack was beyond responding, he might still hear them. They each took time privately and then gathered to pray, their small family circled around a husband and father tethered to machines. Jack's chest rose forcefully and rhythmically, the vent giving the illusion of robust breathing. They

finished praying and stepped out while the breathing tube was removed. Jack never took another breath.

My aunt had died a long time before that long night I spent with
Jack and his wife in the ICU, but her wisdom remained. Remembering
Marianne's unequivocal response, my job was clear. I was there to help
Jack's wife and kids claim this precious gift: sacred time to say goodbye.

Habit of resilience

SAYING LAST WORDS

You may have heard the statistic: More people are afraid of public
speaking than dying. But how about when we combine the two,
speaking about dying to those near death? From my experience, the
idea of speaking to those near death conjures dread. We don't know
what to say; knowing these may be our last words to someone we
love weighs heavily.

Years ago, someone shared with me six simple things to say when
someone is dying. They are: I love you. Thank you. I forgive you.
Forgive me. I (We) will be okay. Goodbye.

Think about your loved one. Consider saying or writing these
thoughts in your own words and style.

1. I love you. Three simple words. Three powerful words. My crusty,
   WWII veteran dad was eighty-eight before he uttered those words
   to me. For years, I'd say "I love you" as I hung up the phone. My
   dad would fumble around and say something like "same here" or
   "I feel the same," but the actual words eluded him until he was on
   his deathbed. Then, remarkably, he said, "I love you."

2. Thank you. I have a thank-you card that reads, "When eating the apple, remember who planted the tree." We don't always remember to thank, and surely we don't often thank the ones who brought us the momentous stuff in our lives: our parents' sacrifice and dedication to make sure we had a chance at a good education; their presence at our band concerts and soccer games; their cheering us on, and seeing the best in us when others saw a different reality. Thank you.

3. I forgive you. Face it. We've all held on to offenses and grudges way too long. Likely, we even remember slights that were not intentional. We hang on to the hurt even though the pain does not serve us well. We allow the pain to be a barrier in our future relationships. Forgiveness does not mean forgetting. It does not mean we are willing to be taken advantage of again. It does mean we are letting go of our options for resentment and revenge as we hand our hurt and anger over to God.

4. Forgive me. The church uses the words "for my sins of omission and commission." Forgive me for what I have done and for what I have failed to do. Sometimes we are more culpable for our inaction than for our action. Can we ask for forgiveness, even if our loved one is no longer able to communicate with us? Asking for forgiveness creates the possibility of forgiveness for some slight or action or word of which we may be completely unaware. Asking for forgiveness allows the dying to impart one final blessing.

5. I will be okay. I am convinced that our loved ones sometimes hang on for us, cling to life because they know we are not yet ready for

them to die. Saying the words "I will be okay" gives your loved one permission to go. When young children are in the picture, let the dying person know that the child will be loved and cared for. Is a parent dying and leaving behind a spouse? Let your parent know you and your siblings will take care of Mom or Dad.

6. Goodbye. Simply letting the dying person know they can go to God when it is their time frees them. Letting go is hard work. But it is also a gift to the dying person. You free them from any sense of obligation to hang on. If they are suffering or in pain, they have your blessing to offer their spirit over to God as Jesus did in his last words, "Father, into your hands I commit my spirit."

Sometimes last conversations bring healing to a relationship that has become defined by wounds and painful history. As John Philip Newell writes, "It is about bringing into relationship again the many parts of our lives, including our brokenness, in order to experience transformation. It is not about forgetting the wound or pretending that it did not happen. It is about seeking a new beginning that grows inseparably from the suffering."[1]

Birthing and dying are oddly similar bedfellows in the circle of life. We had no ideas on how to be born, but we allowed others around us to welcome us into the world. The same can be said of dying. I've noticed that the most peaceful person in the room is often the one dying. As Carl Jung reminds

---

1   J. Philip Newell, *A New Harmony: The Spirit, the Earth, and the Human Soul* (New York: John Wiley & Sons, 2011), p. 99.

us, "Wholeness is about integration…but not perfection."[2] What we say doesn't need to be perfect. Just say it with love.

REFLECTION

Think of the people you love the most in your life. Imagine you are sitting next to them at their deathbed. What would you most want to tell them? If this is something you've never told them, what is holding you back from telling them now?

Think of something you've wanted to share with someone, something you've held back because you didn't want to be hurtful or judgmental. Say it aloud to yourself. Is it something that would bring healing and reconciliation to your relationship? Can you say it in a gentle and loving way? If you can't yet say it to the person who needs to hear this, can you share it first with a trusted friend?

---

2   Newell, ibid., p. 99.

❦ 2 ❦

RESILIENCE IN
THE WAITING TIME

When we were in our twenties, my husband was diagnosed with an insignificant heart murmur, nothing that would ever need surgery, or so we were told. Decades passed; doctors continued to tell us there was no need to worry—until there was.

My sister-in-law, Lisa, had been a critical care cardiac RN. She knew a lot about the procedure Steve was undergoing, enough to be worried. But I was a chaplain and had worked primarily in neurological units. I lived in willful ignorance and had not anticipated critical details, like how long my husband should be on the heart bypass machine. Lisa mentioned in passing that she hoped Steve would be on the bypass fewer than sixty minutes. When the pager hanging from my neck registered sixty-plus minutes on bypass, then seventy-plus minutes, Lisa and I both discarded our Sudoku puzzles and stared down at the pager as the minutes ticked away.

We both grew very quiet. I didn't want to know what she knew. I knew my ignorance wouldn't protect me in this moment, but her information wouldn't either. So I started to breathe and pray.

When my pager finally buzzed at ninety-nine minutes, Lisa and I both let out an enormous breath of relief.

Habit of resilience

PRAY THE BREATH PRAYER

There are times when prayer seems almost beyond our reach. We are mute. There are no words. Our mind sees only darkness. As Thomas Merton reminds us, "Pure love and prayer are learned in the hour when prayer has become impossible and your heart has turned to stone."[3] With this in mind, I offer a version of the breath prayer.

The breath prayer is one of the simplest prayers I know. You can pray this any place, standing, sitting, on a gurney heading into surgery, in the first pew of the church at the funeral of your loved one—any place.

Make yourself comfortable. If possible, sit in a comfortable position with your feet flat on the ground. Close your eyes and notice your breath. Inhale deeply. Fill your lungs completely. With one hand placed on your abdomen, you should feel your belly expand. This deep breathing is sometimes called belly breathing. Inhale through your nose and exhale through your mouth.

With each inhalation, gather the people who love you in your mind. Inhale deep gratitude for their love and support in your life. And as you exhale, let go of whatever fear or worry you are holding. Inhale again, remembering someone else in your circle who has loved and nurtured you. This person does not need to be alive; it can be someone from your past—a parent, grandparent, fabulous aunt, or your favorite teacher. Inhale, filling your whole body with gratitude for their presence in your life, and exhale your anxiety. Simply let it go. Imagine

---

3   Quoted in Joan Chittister, *Listen with the Heart: Sacred Moments in Everyday Life* (Lanham, MO: Rowman and Littlefield, 2003), p. 39.

you can see your breath like vapor on a cold day. Watch your fears and anxiety vanish as the vapor dissipates. Just let it go.

Continue to inhale deeply, inviting the presence of the divine to fill you completely. Exhale. Simply let the thoughts vanish in thin air.

Reflection

One of the games we played with our children was to ask, "Who loves you?" They would start with the simple and obvious: "Mama, Daddy." Then we would ask, "Who else?" and they added names of people in their lives who loved and affirmed them. If you were to imagine a circle of loving support around you, who would be in that circle?

Fear has a way of channeling our thoughts toward the black abyss of grim future possibilities. When you find yourself worrying about unlikely and dreadful future scenarios, what has helped you break this cycle of thinking?

❊ 3 ❊

RESILIENCE WHEN TALKING TO CHILDREN ABOUT DYING

One morning, Dad woke me up for school. My California grand-mother was visiting and he wanted all of us to be extra quiet to let her sleep. Dad never woke us up for school; in fact, he was never in the house when we got up. He was long gone on the train to New York City by the time we climbed out of bed; only in hindsight did this wake-up call seem odd.

When I returned home from school, the house was eerily quiet. No one was home, just a big, empty house. Finally, my older brother shared the devastating news: my Uncle Dwight and Cousin Scotty had been killed in a plane crash. That was it. No other news, no note on the table, nothing but radio silence.

My parents' decision to shelter us from this tragic news did not feel like shelter. I felt utterly alone. I was on the East Coast while they head-ed to California where my grandmother, aunt, and uncle lived. At ten, I was trying to take in the enormity of this loss, but my parents' unspo-ken signals were clear: We were not going to talk about this.

I do not think my parents were alone in their belief that children should be protected from death. But who can truly protect any of us from death? My siblings and I had not attended my grandfather's funeral nine months earlier, and it was clear by my parents' stealth departure we would not attend our uncle and cousin's funeral either. My older siblings fed us and got us on the school bus, but at sixteen and eighteen, they were hardly equipped to deal with my grief much less their own.

If only processing grief could be done well in silence and isolation. But even silence has its own pernicious way of creating meaning, and the meaning I drew out as a child was not that my parents had tenaciously protected my childhood. Rather, it was that there were some things we would never speak of, and death was at the top of that list.

Not giving voice to the tragic events in my life did not diminish their impact; their shadows only grew larger. It was the silence that gave power to these events. Failure to name the pain created a stumbling block, leaving me poorly equipped even to recognize my painful or difficult emotions.

The following summer, my Aunt Marianne and two cousins came to Connecticut to visit. Leaving the airport, someone noticed a plane with a badly damaged nose cone. "Maybe it was in an accident," I said without thinking. My mother shot me a look so powerfully angry it frightened me. But I got the message: plane accidents were on the list of unspeakable things.

My husband told me a story of a woman who shared openly with her three-year-old grandchild as her brother's cancer progressed. Glenda was heading to California through Minneapolis, when she ended up in the last row of the plane sitting next to my husband. She'd been the primary caretaker for her younger brother, who had died recently. As her story unfolded, it became clear that she understood a couple of things very clearly: children are in relationship with God, and sometimes children can teach us more about death than we can teach them.

Glenda's brother Dell had been diagnosed with cancer in July of 2006. After successful treatment, Dell was reportedly cancer free. He went on to live another seven years. In that time, Glenda's daughter delivered Glenda's first and only grandchild, Jayden. Glenda helped with childcare.

Dell lived with Glenda, and Jayden became his attentive companion. The two became good buddies. When Dell got sick, doctors confirmed what no one wanted to hear. Dell's cancer was back. Glenda had made a promise to her parents and to her older brother that she would look after Dell, and she fulfilled her promise with grace and dignity. She told Dell, "I will be your eyes, ears, and voice. I will be there to the end." She did more than advocate for him; she did his laundry; she visited him every day once he went into hospice; and she allowed Jayden to be part of this journey.

Jayden, his little mascot, accompanied Dell to every radiation appointment and every visit to the oncologist. He spent visits climbing on Dell's bed, exchanging high fives and shadow boxing. He had no hesitation in telling Dell he needed to clean out his tracheotomy tube and wipe his nose. "That is nasty," he would say with the earnestness of a three-year-old.

Jayden also had no hesitation asking hard questions and wondering out loud about what was happening. Jayden wanted to know why Dell was in a wheelchair. What had happened to Dell? Was Dell going to die? Glenda told him everybody's going to die one day. As Dell got worse, Jayden took his case to the doctors and nurses. "Can you fix Dell?" he would ask. The nurses answered honestly, "We can help him feel better."

Dell was in hospice for a month before he died. Jayden saw Dell get progressively sicker. He told his "Granny," as he called Glenda, that he was going to pray for Dell to get better.

The day before Dell died, Glenda and Jayden stayed for an unusually long visit. When they started to leave, Jayden returned and whispered something in Dell's ear. Dell had lost his voice in the last couple of weeks, but this didn't deter Jayden. Again they turned to leave and Jayden returned. He told Dell, "You're going to be all right. Jesus will take care of you. You aren't going to hurt anymore." And then Jayden did something he hadn't done before: he kissed Dell goodbye. Dell, with his tracheotomy tube and cancer on his mouth and snot coming out his nose (as Jayden liked to remind him), was not a likely candidate for kisses. But there it was, a kiss goodbye from Dell's precious little buddy. Dell died before sunrise the next morning.

Glenda said, "My brother was waiting for Jayden to let go. He was waiting for Jayden to give him permission."

Jayden has turned four since his Uncle Dell died. He has asked to watch the video of Uncle Dell's funeral a couple of times. He's processing his Uncle Dell's death with concrete, direct questions, wondering if all the people in the cemetery are asleep in their little houses. He's announced when he grows up he wants to become a doctor.

Glenda did more than honor her pledge to be her brother's eyes, ears, and voice. She did more than stay with him until the end, watching as Dell's casket was lowered into the ground and covered with dirt. Glenda journeyed with her brother and her young grandson, letting both know that death is a part of life. She did not discourage Jayden when he jumped on Dell's bed, rubbed his knees and his arms, and told him to "clean your nose; you look nasty." She did not shush him or hustle him out when he repeatedly went back to whisper one more goodbye. In the end, it was Jayden who knew when to say, "You are going to be all right. Jesus will take care of you."

Habit of resilience

BE OPEN, NOT SILENT

Our silence does not stop a child from trying to make meaning out of painful circumstances. Rudolf Dreikurs, the educator and psychiatrist, was quoted as saying that children are keen observers but poor interpreters.[4]

Children have a way of asking questions adults are afraid to ask or answer. Jayden asked simple, concrete questions. Could the doctors "fix" Dell? Ultimately, Glenda gave Jayden priceless gifts: the right to feel sad, and the chance to say goodbye. And Jayden returned the favor, reminding us that, in spite of our snot, we are all beloved children of God.

REFLECTION

We cannot change our family history, but we don't have to repeat it. As you think about how your family approached difficult subjects, what would you want to change?

Children often show very different responses to grief. Adults sometimes believe children are fine simply because their grief response differs so radically from adults. Talking to children can help identify delayed or unexpected grief responses in children. Are there children in your life? Who is able to broach the difficult topic of death and loss with them if needed?

---

4   Quoted in Jan Silvious, *Same Life, New Story: Change Your Perspective to Change Your Life* (Nashville: Thomas Nelson, 2010), p. 33.

❦ 4 ❦

RESILIENCE IN
DECISION MAKING

Years ago, I was called into a care conference for an eighty-six-year-old man who had suffered a massive stroke. He was not expected to survive, and the family needed to make some difficult decisions about his care, including whether to allow him to undergo surgery to place a feeding tube since he was no longer able to swallow. It soon became clear I was not invited there to process grief and loss, but to help with family mediation. The room was packed with a dozen or more adults in their thirties and forties and one older woman: the many sons and daughters (and spouses) and their stepmom.

It's no wonder stepmoms have been maligned in our imagination, with Cinderella and Snow White providing the backdrop for wicked stepmom myths. I'd like to say this stepmom was maligned as well, but unfortunately, she stepped fully into her role as a conniving woman, willing to serve her own needs ruthlessly. From the outset, it was clear Margaret had claimed her sole authority as next of kin. She had the legal right to make any medical decisions for her husband, and she had no intention of sharing her decision-making authority with her stepchildren, who clearly loved and cared for him too.

Normally, this would have made the care conference a moot point, but the patient's adult children, his medical team, and his health care directive leaned clearly in one direction, and his wife stood as the outlier leaning the opposite way.

The situation was ironic: Margaret could only wield the power to make medical decisions for her husband because he had been deemed significantly cognitively impaired after his stroke. But she argued that he was not impaired, and she insisted that he had spoken to her and verbally requested the feeding tube.

The stroke had complicated his care. Physicians were unsure from moment to moment whether the patient fully understood what was going on, and what choice he was making. Cognitive impairment is not uncommon with stroke, and all indications suggested this was a real concern for the patient. The staff had been able to rouse him with great effort but was only able to elicit yes or no responses. All too frequently, he responded to the same question with both a yes and a no answer, leaving the medical staff no option but to turn to his wife for guidance. With the glaring exception of his wife, all in the room were quite concerned that this patient had no idea where he was or what they were asking. But Margaret insisted her husband knew what he wanted and that he wanted a feeding tube. She peppered this with barbs like "You never really loved your father" and "You don't know him like I do."

To their credit, his children never took the bait in her one-sided fight. In an attempt to de-escalate the deteriorating care conference, we mutually agreed to have Margaret and me speak to the patient. When we went in, Margaret spoke to her husband, reminding him he could no longer swallow and would need a feeding tube to eat. Did he want a feeding tube? He turned to her, looked her in the eye, and said, "No."

She immediately shot back to me, "He doesn't know what he's saying." As soon as she said this, she realized she had just confirmed what his children and doctors had been saying—her husband really had no clue what she was asking, who she was, or why she was in the room. She asked again. "No," he said firmly. She was fuming. His refusal of the feeding tube or sheer confusion had left her in an untenable position with her stepchildren, whom she felt had mistreated her for years. She announced she would not return to the care conference.

She was so entrenched in her fight with his children that she was unable to re-engage. His emphatic "no" had undermined her contention that she knew best. Instead of letting in the possibility that others loved her husband too and wanted what was best for him, she chose to make the decision alone.

She used her trump card as next of kin and in doing so she bucked the entire family, the written instructions of her husband, and the medical advice of his physicians, who felt the patient was high risk for this or any other procedure. Yet, she clearly felt she had "won"; at her request, the patient received a feeding tube, never regained consciousness after the procedure, and died two days later. In the two-day vigil, she refused to allow any of his children into the hospital room. His kids wondered whether she might bury him in secret, not next to their mother as he had requested but in a plot of her choosing. She had spectacularly achieved the title I suspect she secretly believed she already was—the hideous stepmom whom no one loved.

A death in the family brings out the best in the family, or the worst. There is often no middle ground. Either siblings and the surviving parent rally to support and affirm one another, or they haul out decades-old grudges and replay their conflicted scripts.

This is why funeral planning is fascinating. The logistics are not particularly difficult, but the family dynamics never fail to amaze. Some families work hard to achieve a consensus, valuing every voice in the room. Others exhibit power dynamics, where one or more siblings actively try to shut other siblings out of the process. In the worst cases, siblings will slander their siblings all under the guise of "what Mom or Dad wanted." I always wonder if those desperately trying to take control of the funeral process felt they had no control or respect as children, and now, decades later, it's payback time.

It's painful to watch and work with some families. Some siblings carry the hurts and grievances that they had as children, never maturing to the point of having a fully adult relationship with their siblings. Their lack of awareness wreaks havoc on the family, occasionally unraveling the very fabric of familial ties. Their hell-bent efforts to exact revenge may briefly put them in a position of power in the family, but it is a brief power play that almost always serves to further isolate them. The emotional immaturity blinds them, and they often spend too much time self-justifying their behavior as "best" for the family. They never accept accountability for their childish, mean-spirited acts—they can't; their lack of self-awareness has left them emotionally crippled, and they are unable to see what the rest of the world cringes at: an adult acting like a petulant child, emotionally incapable of entering into a collaborative process.

Thankfully, there is another side to loss, the side where grace appears. At the very same hospital, I faced a strikingly similar situation. A woman in her mid-forties had a massive stroke. The family gathered in the ICU to consider some of the difficult decisions ahead. Her husband and three young adult children sat at one table as the doctor explained the seriousness of her situation. She was in grave danger, and even the most aggressive treatment might not save her. As the options and risks were discussed, the husband continued to defer to the adult children. "What do you want to do?" he would say. "I really want to do what you all would want for your mom." His respectful demeanor and collaborative decision making made it possible for all the kids to voice their hopes and their fears for their mom.

I just listened. Even when dissenting opinions were voiced, others listened. Everyone was able to voice the tough, scary feelings that accompanied these wrenching decisions; everything was on the table. It had taken nearly an hour for me to realize that the husband was also a stepdad. Like the stepmom, he too clearly understood that he had the legal right to decide. He also had the grace to invite others into this painful time of goodbye.

Habit of resilience

Honor relationships by listening

Compassionate decision making requires self-awareness of our particular worldview. This may sound simple. But we don't always consciously consider our point of view as just that—one point of view among many. Sometimes we believe so strongly that we are right that we cannot imagine others holding a thoughtful alternative opinion. We are so intent on presenting our point of view that we fail to listen to another point of view.

To make compassionate and wise choices, we need to listen with the intent to understand. We may not agree. But if we understand, we stand a chance of making a compassionate choice.

Collaborative decision making is a skill. Collaboration does not *de facto* mean compromise. It means listening to multiple points of view and collectively crafting the best solution from the wisdom of the group. It presupposes two things: we value the opinions of others, and we recognize that we don't have all the answers. When we invite others into dialogue, we acknowledge that ours is just one perspective among many.

Listening honors another person's story. In honoring their story, we let them know we value our relationship with them. In the end, life is always about relationships.

REFLECTION

Think of someone you admire, someone who makes wise and compassionate decisions. How would you describe their decision making? What distinguishes them as a role model for you?

Think of those who value their relationship with you. What do they do or say to let you know they value you? Do you feel heard? Do they seek your opinion?

If your family dynamics are difficult and laden with painful history, what will you do to seek health and wholeness? If your parents have held together a contentious family, what sort of relationship do you want with your siblings or other family members when your last parent dies?

Staying resilient for others

✠ 5 ✠

If one part suffers, all the parts suffer with it;
if one part is honored, all the parts share its joy.

1 CORINTHIANS 12:26

SUPPORT RESILIENCE THROUGH COMMUNITY: THE CUT TEAM

Friday, February 28, 2014, was an ordinary day in Minnesota. A week earlier, a wintery mix had covered the state with several inches of slush. The slush froze into a solid slab of ice and was soon covered with a foot of snow. Although the snow was plowed from the roads, little could be done to clear the ice, and driving had been treacherous all week. Subzero temperatures continued, making salt and chemicals ineffective at melting the ice, and poor road conditions lingered. The weather report for February 28 was all too familiar: Minnesota was slated for another visit from the polar vortex in a winter that wouldn't end. Road conditions would be complicated by high winds, blowing snow, and reduced visibility.

Early that Friday morning, members of the Carleton College Ultimate Frisbee Team began ferrying teammates along the forty-mile drive from Carleton to the Minneapolis/St. Paul Airport. The Ultimate Frisbee Team, dubbed CUT for Carleton Ultimate Team, was scheduled to play in an invitational tournament the next day at

Stanford University in California. Most of the team members had afternoon flights, and although the day had begun cold and clear, the weather was deteriorating as the drivers returned to campus to pick up additional carloads of teammates.

Shortly before 1:00 PM, whiteout conditions northwest of campus triggered a fifty-car pileup on Interstate Highway 35. With the usual route to the airport unexpectedly closed, team members loaded into three cars and headed north on State Highway 3, a smaller, less traveled two-lane road. James Patrick Adams and four others were in the third vehicle, a Toyota 4Runner. Four were CUT teammates; the driver was a friend.

A few miles north of campus, the 4Runner hit a patch of ice, spun into oncoming traffic, and slammed head-on into a semi-trailer truck. James Adams, Paxton Harvieux, and Michael Goodgame died at the scene. The driver and another teammate were hospitalized; one was airlifted to a Minneapolis trauma hospital, and the other was transported there after his condition was stabilized at a regional hospital.

According to the state police, neither speeding nor alcohol played a role in the accident. All five were wearing seat belts. Five young men were doing everything right, and then without warning, everything went horribly wrong. James was buried a week before his twenty-first birthday.

Team members and family friends described James as a kid that sparkled: academically gifted, a natural leader, and a scholar-athlete. James was a Minnesotan. He'd canoed the Boundary Waters and north each summer through high school, culminating in a Voyager trip through YMCA Camp Widjiwagan to Northern Canada and Hudson Bay. James Adams's obituary and those of his two teammates, Michael Goodgame and Paxton Harvieux, all spoke to the talent, potential, and accomplishment of these three young men.

When tragedies like this happen, how do we move on? How do we face the next ordinary day in our lives, when it seems nothing will ever be ordinary again? There are no right answers, yet one parent commented that Carleton College "did everything right." What did Carleton do, and why did it resonate?

Carleton held a prayer vigil on campus the day after the accident, and it planned a service to be held in April 2014. Carleton kept updating information on the accident on its website, with links to obituaries, funeral details, and forums to express condolences. From the beginning, their message was clear: we're in this together, and we will not forget. The college funded travel expenses for the entire Ultimate team to attend the funeral of Michael Goodgame in Westport, Connecticut.

Carleton tapped into their tradition of "Friday Flowers," where anyone can purchase a flower and tuck it in a student mailbox. One week after the tragic car accident and the day after the first funeral, volunteers stayed up all night to wrap white roses in paper with a note of love and encouragement and to tuck them into every single Carleton student mailbox.

Carleton is a small college, and the gesture was extended to the entire student body, not just to an exclusive group like the CUT teammates or fellow dorm members. This loss hurt the entire community, not just the friends and teammates of those who died.

The white rose was more than a symbol of their grief; a white rose also has come to symbolize an everlasting and eternal love that is stronger than death. By giving the rose, the Carleton community symbolically named the loss for each student and the entire community. Despite the frigid weather, white roses were seen peeking out of backpacks and messenger bags, a visible reminder of the community's loss.

Carleton arranged buses on the day of the Minnesota funerals. Some days, buses are merely transportation. Not this day. Students traveled as a community of grievers, not as isolated individuals. Surely this was the first death of a peer for many. Carleton's response helped show these students that grief is normal. We do not like it. It is gut wrenchingly painful, but it is normal.

Carleton was not the only community to reach out. Ultimate Frisbee is a tight-knit community. Players know each other, playing with and against each other for years. Cards, letters, and online posts flooded in, not merely for the families but also for the CUT team. Dartmouth College Ultimate Frisbee sent CUT a note of condolence on a signed Ultimate Disc. Whitman College posted remembrances; online Ultimate forums exploded with memorial postings. Ultimate Frisbee's small community felt the searing pain from coast to coast.

Ultimate Frisbee teams around the country made a video condolence card for the CUT team and posted it on a private YouTube channel. Each team recited one verse of a poem titled "For Our Brothers and Sisters," reminding CUT that the Ultimate world shared in their loss. It was a reminder that we are profoundly connected.

Scott Boehm was one of many non-Carleton Ultimate players who traveled to James's visitation. A Luther College Ultimate player, Scott had met James at a tournament in Milwaukee. It was a fortuitous meeting. During a match, Scott was kneed in the chest. His heart stopped. This rare occurrence occurs when there is impact over the heart at a particular point in the heart rhythm. Reports vary on how long it took the sheriff to arrive; some say five to seven minutes; others reported over eleven minutes. What is not in dispute is that James was one of the players who assisted with CPR so that Scott might live to play another game. CPR saved Scott through those long minutes waiting for help. When the sheriff arrived with the automated external defibrillator, a shock and some additional chest compressions got Scott's heart going again. Scott came to James's visitation with a heartfelt message; he knew the thin line between life and death and was indebted to James for his very life.

Someone placed three white crosses on Highway 3, a visible reminder of the tragedy. The mother of one player, a woman who might describe herself as spiritual but not religious, spoke about how difficult it was for the team to drive past the crosses. As one of two main routes north, team members would pass this spot often before graduation. She wondered what kind of ritual the team might adopt to honor their dead teammates each time they passed this spot. Even someone who rarely if ever enters a church recognized this place as holy ground.

A flower, a bus ride, or an online post: all tiny but important first steps in the long and anguished journey of grief. Recovery is not the flower, bus ride, or post. Resilience comes from a caring community that ultimately helps us on our journey through grief.

The young Carleton players will carry their deceased teammates throughout their lives. My husband lost a teammate in college; his friend died while cross-country skiing near his home in Boston. His skis got tangled in the rails at a train crossing, and he was unable to free himself before being hit by a train. At the Unitarian funeral, the young man's father closed his eulogy by saying, "Now, Chase only lives on in the memories of those of us who knew him." It's been thirty-eight years, and my husband says that when the intercessions are prayed for the dead at his church, invariably he thinks of Chase.

At James's funeral, his father told the team he wanted the young men to stay in touch with him—not just this year and next while James would have been a Carleton student, but when they get their first job, get married, and have a family. He said he wanted to stay connected to James through his connection with the team. When the unthinkable happens, these invitations to connection offer us the strength to bear the unbearable.

Habit of resilience

LIVE AN INTERCONNECTED LIFE

Traumatic events have a greater capacity to foster a sense of connectedness. Tornados, 9/11, floods, hurricanes—they all remind us that we are in this together. Recognizing our deep interconnectedness helps us respond and receive compassion. Journeying together helps us share the burdens and lightens our load.

But not all of our losses are traumatic and garner a public outpouring of grief. Our connectedness may not be so obvious to us or to others. We may have to work harder to develop an awareness of our interconnectedness.

Some find a sense of connectedness by joining a grief group, returning to a faith community, or finding strong listening support. People in grief groups seem to speak the same language. They understand what you are going through and can hear your story in ways others simply can't. Faith communities are better equipped to engage with questions of life and death. And listening support—who can't use the ear of a compassionate listener?

REFLECTION

Where do you feel the deepest sense of connection in your life? Faith community, family, grief support group, nature?

Remembering your own grief, what were the meaningful gestures that touched your heart?

❦ 6 ❦

SUPPORT RESILIENCE
BY OPENING THE CIRCLE
OF GRIEVING

Last winter, my women's group headed north to the National Forest Lodge in Isabella, Minnesota, for a snowshoe/cross-country ski weekend. Way back in September before the leaves turned, we thought that the last weekend in February might be dicey for skiing. We worried about having enough snow to cross-country ski and snowshoe. Why is it that the things we worry about rarely come to pass, and the things we never consider loom large?

For safety reasons, we employed the buddy system. There was so much snow when we arrived that we needed help after a wipeout to climb out of the deep drifts and get back onto the trail. It was also cold, really cold. Our last day out, the temperature was -26˚F. You'd have to be either a self-righteous fool or a blithering idiot to go out in those conditions. Count me in.

The trip was a "plus one" event. We wanted the lodge, which had a distinct advantage over the rustic cabins available for smaller groups: indoor plumbing. This required a larger group, and several of us immediately invited our "plus one," guaranteeing the requisite flush toilets. I invited my daughter Sarah.

This was our first "plus one" event in years. Three and a half years before, on another of our adventures, our friend Lisa Roden was killed in a bike accident. Lisa was arguably one of the fittest in the group and an avid cyclist. What started out as an ordinary women's group outing on a perfect August evening ended in gut-wrenching tragedy. Lisa and another cyclist hit head-on as Lisa entered a tunnel on the bike path. In the collision, Lisa's helmet was pulled down towards her face. When she was thrown off the bike, her helmet was no longer on her head. She died of a traumatic brain injury later that night.

The group, dubbed "the sisterhood," has discovered more about grief than we ever wanted. Painfully, we learned that grief has no time-table. If we didn't know it before, we knew it now. Everyone grieves differently. There is no right way to grieve, and the most loving gift we have given each other is a non-judgmental stance to grieve Lisa in the way each of us must.

We have learned this the hard way. Some leave flowers at Lisa's grave or call her mom for an occasional dinner out. Each of us has taken a day of the week to remember Lisa in prayer. Others grieve in less visible ways.

Remember those great movie scenes of a dying person in the embrace of another, asking them to pass on a message of eternal love to their husband and children? That didn't happen. Lisa was gentle and affirming; she often spoke about her family with tenderness and love. I have no doubt her last words would have been words of love for her family. But there were no last words; Lisa never got the chance. She hit the ground and was never responsive again.

Our reality teetered between unspeakable pain and magical denial in the face of Lisa's death. The miraculous time-traveling denial lobe of our brains wasn't looking for a loving goodbye. We wanted more. We wanted to rewind the clock back to the sliver of time before

Lisa collided head-on with another cyclist. We wanted the vibrant, creative, artistic Lisa back. We spent more time than I'd like to admit playing "what if" and "if only," remembering that Lisa had first floated the idea of the bike outing. And Lisa had changed the date on short notice. Instead of leaving from Lisa's house on a familiar bike path, Lisa had thrown her bike and helmet into her truck and met the group at a different, less familiar trail. What if one small, tiny detail of that day had been different? But none of our ranting or wishes changed our sad and harsh reality. Our darling, sweet Lisa was dead.

To say we tightened the circle after Lisa's death is an understatement. We didn't know how to welcome a newcomer into our pain. Somehow, adding someone new to our women's group felt strangely disloyal to Lisa, as if we were moving on without her. Slowly, over the course of years, Lisa's death became a sacred part of our story, but not our entire story, which brings me to the ski trip.

The ski trip was a new chapter in our grief, a breakthrough weekend of sorts. It was our first trip inviting others into a circle of women who have nurtured and supported each other through our kids' growing up times: high school and college graduations; job changes; marriages of our kids; the deaths of our parents; a newly minted PhD; and most searing for the group, Lisa's death.

Although none of us discussed whom we planned to invite, we all chose family, sisters, and daughters who had witnessed our painful goodbye from a distance. Vicky's sister came, the sister who went biking with Vicky shortly after Lisa's death and stopped to watch how Vicky was coping as she approached her first bike tunnel. My daughter Sarah came. Sarah has known most of the sisterhood since she was three. She celebrated my fiftieth birthday by cooking a French meal for me and the sisterhood, with my husband as her sous chef.

The sisterhood has watched Sarah grow up and come into her own as a young adult. And she has watched us.

Sarah sent me a note shortly after the trip. It read:

> *Dear Mom,*
>
> *Thank you so much for including me in your women's ski weekend up north! I had such a good time catching up with you on our drive north, hanging out in the cozy cabin, skiing among the beautiful pines, and resting my sore muscles on the drive home. Most of all, it was so special to see what a strong support network you have with the sisterhood. I hope I am as lucky to have a strong group of women in my life.*
>
> *I love you, Sarah*

I sent her this response.

> *Dear Sarah,*
>
> *I hope you are blessed with strong women in your life too. I hope you can find women you can trust to hold your fears and dreams close to their hearts, women who can love you in spite of yourself, and women who have the courage to tell you the truth when you need to hear it. I've often thought this is why Jesus sent the disciples out in twos. Everyone needs a buddy. When you go headfirst into the snowdrifts of life, I hope you have people who love you enough to help dig you out, dust you off, and set your skis on the trail again.*
>
> *I love you, Mom*

Our snowy winter of new beginnings gave way to a late spring.

Hesitantly, almost four years after the accident, we went biking again as a group. Another first, and another reminder that grief has no time-table. When the trail crossed a busy thoroughfare, we stopped and walked our bikes across the crosswalk. I have no doubt each one of us was quietly remembering Lisa. We are moving on, but not without Lisa. She rode alongside us for a while, and now she has gone ahead.

Habit of resilience

PASS ON YOUR LIFE LESSONS BY OPENING THE CIRCLE OF GRIEF
While shopping for outdoor furniture, I noticed an inscription carved in a bench. It said, "It takes a long time to grow old friends." This inscription could have been written for my women's group. Most of us have known each other for decades. We have raised our babies together and watched them grow up and begin families of their own.

As one friend said, "You have earned the right to speak into my life." Some of us, if we are lucky, find ourselves in the company of others who have earned the right to speak into our lives. Deep friendships ground us. Good friends are a calming and healing presence when our world turns upside down. Friends help us recognize the ebb and flow of life and lend a hand to help us stay balanced. Friends are a rich blessing.

But the richness of this blessing is not for me alone, nor for my friends or yours. Luke's gospel reminds us that the blessings bestowed on us come with an expectation: "From everyone who has been given much, much will be required" (Luke 12:48). We are called to be both blessed and blessing to others.

How we pass on the blessings in our life is, in part, up to us. One woman whose precious daughter was killed in a tragic car accident has gone on to coordinate her area's grief support group. She recognized the blessing of the grief group. When she felt ready, she volunteered her time as coordinator of the grief group. Years ago, they were a steadying hand in her time of need. Now, she reaches out her hand to others.

Perhaps you don't feel ready yet. I understand. Believe me, my women's group has taken baby steps to pass it on, to widen the circle. Some day you will look back and realize that this time of deep grief has prepared you to be a blessing for someone else.

REFLECTION

Have you ever played the "what if" and "if only" game in your head, imagining changing one small thing in the past that would change your current reality too?

Finish this sentence: "I knew I was making progress in my grief journey when_____."

❧ 7 ❧

SUPPORT RESILIENCE
BY BEING PRESENT

My pager sounded, and I looked down to see the page from Children's Hospital. I hated covering Children's. Losing a child is one of my deepest fears. It's the one loss I am not sure I would recover from. I have precious children of my own, plus nephews, nieces, and exchange students who are family; these calls cut too close to the bone. What could I possibly say that would offer comfort or compassion to a grieving parent at such an agonizing moment?

I called the hospital to let them know when they could expect me, and also to get some sense of the situation I was about to walk into. The early news was very tough. A two-month-old infant had arrived from Iowa by helicopter. The mother was young and single. When I cleared the emergency department door, I could hear her wailing, "This can't be happening." She cried this same phrase again and again and again as if to take in the enormity of the situation.

As I rounded the corner, I saw a sea of scrubs: a medical team of twenty or more surrounding this nine-pound infant.

As I approached the mother and reached out to comfort her, she recoiled, and I felt her rage and anger aimed directly toward me. I soon discovered why.

Her baby boy was a preemie. The mother was still a teen and the child's father was in the military, not present for the child's birth and not present now. The birth and early days had been complicated by more than the premature delivery; the mother was an addict. The infant had been born an addict too, and had several seizures in his early days—"little tremors," his mother called them. In normal circumstances, the mother would have lost custody. But she was in a methadone clinic and was no longer addicted to heroin. Now she was addicted to methadone. This was considered part of her treatment plan, and baby Jeremy's addiction was collateral damage.

The good news was that she could keep Jeremy; the bad news was that she could keep Jeremy. This was a poster child for an infant at risk: born to an addict, no father present, and a maternal grandmother who had kicked the mother out in tough love demanding she get clean or get out. Her boyfriend, on a six-month deployment that promised to be longer, had only seen their child in photos taken from her phone. She had one thing in the world that she could cling to: this fragile, medically needy little boy.

Despite his rocky start, Jeremy made steady progress, and all the early indicators suggested he was thriving. She was nursing the baby successfully, and the baby was nearly nine pounds at two months.

A few days before the emergency helicopter ride, the mother had been encouraged by her baby's pediatrician to begin the baby on formula in an effort to boost his weight. From the start, the mother sensed something was wrong. She called, explained what was going on with her son, and was rebuffed by the nurses. When her baby seemed worse, she called again. This time the nurse, thinking she had put the mom on hold, said, "It's just that young mom again." Unbeknownst to the nurse, the mom had heard the nurse's dismissive comment. As she shared this, our eyes briefly met. There was no sadness, only pure hate at the thoughtlessness of a nurse who had failed to take a mother's cry for help seriously.

By the time the infant was examined at a hospital in Iowa, it was apparent something was seriously wrong. Concerned that the baby was dying, the hospital made the decision to airlift the mother and child to a level 1 hospital. From the moment the infant was rushed into the emergency department until they pronounced the child dead, no effort was spared trying to stabilize the infant. But the infant never stabilized over the course of that long day, and one by one his internal organs began to fail.

The doctor, a male, came out to speak with the mom, and she trusted him. The news was not good, and he had clearly taken time to come out to establish some rapport, knowing he would likely be delivering more difficult news later that day.

As this situation unfolded, I noticed another young man in the emergency department. His infant daughter was being treated; she was also likely to die. Like the young mother, he was also enraged; his daughter had been shaken by the child's mother, his estranged partner. He ranted about a system that favored custody of the mother when clearly she had grievously harmed his child, their child. A local news report came on the TV. "That's me," he said. I looked up and there he was, being interviewed by a local reporter. He seemed pleased that his baby girl's injury was newsworthy and that others were outraged too.

When the baby died, the mother would be charged with murder. This, it seemed, was what he wanted more than anything. I did not want to tell him that this revenge would be little solace for his empty arms, for the daughter he would never take to kindergarten or walk down the aisle at her wedding. A mistake made in a moment of sheer frustration from a stressed-out, overtired mom—these are the things that would reverberate for the rest of his life, a forever loss. Making his ex-girlfriend wrong would never change the outcome for this beautiful baby girl.

Like the angry young mother, he was alone, and they made an immediate connection. Both had been wronged by "the system." Both were wary as feral cats of any offer of emotional or spiritual support.

Later that afternoon, he rebuffed me directly, scolding me for not providing much-needed solace to this young mom from Iowa. A piece of me wanted righteously to defend myself, to point out that I was tarred with the brush of some thoughtless nurse 300 miles away and a tough-love mother. But another part of me knew he was right. I had not been able to reach her, to break through her anger toward a system that had failed her and her infant son so tragically.

I felt completely stuck and useless. Hospital protocol demanded that I stay until the infant was either stabilized and admitted or dead. But I was less helpful than a fifth wheel, unable to penetrate her anger and rage and, I suspect, her belief that she had been judged and found unworthy.

I was worse than useless; my mere presence conjured all the harsh, insensitive women in her life that had cast her out to fend for herself. I desperately wanted to leave, and I had concocted a compelling story in my mind about how it would be better for her if I was not present. Not coincidentally, it would have been a lot easier for me too.

When Jeremy died, the doctor broke the news to the young mother as gently as he could. We sat with her and listened to all the interventions he had tried in vain. He sat with her as I accompanied a nurse to cut a short lock of hair and to take Jeremy's hand and foot print, keepsakes of a child who died too soon. Jeremy was battered and bruised from his day in the hospital after countless attempts to restart his heart and find veins for medications. Every inch of his torso and his tiny arms was covered in dark blue bruises. I did not want the mother to see her son for the last time like this, a grim reminder that all the hours of pushing and prodding to hold back death had been futile.

We wrapped Jeremy tightly in a couple of blankets and placed him in her arms. I began to silently plead with God, "Please, please, please, do not let her unwrap the blankets." It was the least I could offer for a young mother who had already been beaten by a system that didn't trust a mother's instincts.

As much as I had wanted to turn on my heel and run out the doors of the hospital earlier, I could not leave now. I felt compelled to stay. How could I leave this mom, so alone and so bereft? When she handed back her dead son, he would go to the morgue, and she would go to a cheap hotel set up by the social worker: alone, in a strange city, arms empty of everything important to her yet still riddled with the needle marks of her past. Everything about this was wrong. I was about to take her son after her last look at this precious child and exchange him for a lock of hair and a footprint.

If ever there was a day that called me to an examination of conscience, this was it. I felt I had mishandled the situation, that my ineptness had left this young woman even more fragile and vulnerable. I was one link in a long chain of medical caregivers who had failed her.

We will never know if the cascading events that ended in this infant boy's death could have been prevented by better and more responsive medical care early on. The circumstances of his life and death were muddled at best; he was a preemie, and he was an addict. His mother was a teen, and while she tried to advocate for him, she did not have the skills to navigate a complicated healthcare system. Her own self-protective lack of trust made it difficult for others to advocate for her. In every way possible, this was one ugly mess, and I was part of that mess.

Habit of resilience

DO A PERSONAL *EXAMEN*

An examination of conscience is that moment of self-awareness and self-reflection when we consider what we have done and what we have failed to do that begs for forgiveness. For Christians, a personal *examen* is always rooted in the Scriptures and provides us with a chance to prayerfully consider our shortcomings.

On days like these, we generally know where we have dropped the ball. I was acutely aware that this young woman was both economically poor and spiritually, physically, and emotionally vulnerable. Had my words and actions empowered her and given her hope? Or, as I feared, had I bumbled my way through what surely was the worst day in her life?

The examination of conscience does more than serve as a guide to where we have failed and what needs forgiveness. It also gives us a chance to consider how we might do a better job tomorrow so that we might wake up and begin again.

Here is my prayer for that day.

> Create in me a clean heart, O God,
> And put a new and right spirit within me.
> Cast me not away from your presence,
> And take not your holy spirit from me.
> Restore to me the joy of your salvation,
> And sustain in me a willing spirit. PSALM 51:10–12

REFLECTION

Sometimes we have no words for unspeakable losses. All we can do is sit with someone in silence and pray. Our presence matters, not our words. Could you sit in silence, just being there, for someone in need?

Sometimes events quickly cascade into chaos and trauma. Often no one person or event is the tipping point. The day unravels with a series of unfortunate events like falling dominoes. When this happens and you know you are not solely or partially responsible, do you stop to consider what you might have done to change the course of the day?

When the day comes that you can do nothing right, when nothing you say is consoling, try to remember this question: What is the best, most noble thing I can do right now?

⌘ 8 ⌘

SUPPORT RESILIENCE:
ASK FOR AND OFFER HELP

When I was seven months pregnant with our second child, my husband announced that he had told his boss he planned to leave the firm soon. He was not looking for a job, had not interviewed, had no obvious prospects, and most importantly for my standpoint, had not discussed this with me.

Pregnant and a stay-at-home mom with an active seventeen-month-old toddler, I was not in a strong position to interview for a job. I was convinced my obvious pregnancy would eliminate me from any serious job consideration. I felt angry and isolated; unilateral decision making had not been a hallmark of our marriage, and no matter how convinced Steve was that this was the right decision, his process felt like a violation of our partnership.

Steve's decision led us into months of chaos. He soon began working two jobs; he continued to work at his old job as part of his commitment to complete any outstanding projects, and he had already started a new job. Both jobs demanded travel, and I remember asking as he packed a suitcase whom he was working for that day.

Sarah was born on a Friday night, giving us the weekend to regroup before Steve's next trip. My mother, a natural caregiver, arrived from the East Coast and stayed for two weeks, cooking, cleaning, doing laundry, and letting me sleep. When she left, I thought we could manage despite Steve's crazy work schedule. Then I came down with chicken pox.

Apparently, I'd had one pox as an infant. My doctor suspected I had developed an incomplete immune response to the chicken pox, enough to get me through my childhood years, but not enough to weather exposure as an adult. Thus began a miserable month of chicken pox; first mine, then two weeks later both my children's.

Chicken pox for a child is aggravating; for an adult it is downright miserable. I had pox from the soles of my feet to my scalp and every imaginable and unimaginable place in between. I counted seventy pox on my forearm one day; the fact that I bothered to count tells you how invested I was in feeling miserable and feeling sorry for myself.

As viruses go, chicken pox is highly contagious. This meant we were essentially housebound for the month. No one needed contagious kids in the grocery store or anywhere else. With Steve traveling, I was left to care for the three of us.

A couple of acquaintances had heard I was home with chicken pox and brought a meal. I was surprised and touched. A friend brought me Tylenol; I was nursing and my doctor didn't want me to have anything stronger. But several friends ignored me for the month. No calls, no helpful meals at the door, no offers of help.

I had plenty of time to nurse a grudge over the perceived lack of compassion I received. I mentally cataloged all the meals I'd prepared, the childcare I'd offered, the many ways I'd cared for friends in need. But never once in all my fuming did I pick up the phone and ask for help.

Some people are natural caregivers, and if you are one of them, I'm guessing you can relate. Seeing what needs to be done and offering help comes naturally to some, but it is neither intuitive nor natural for others. While some people seem to know just what to say and what help to offer, others are oblivious. And sometimes, it is those who seem to have a double dose of empathy who feel frustrated when others do not perceive their needs. This may be because the person who helps others so easily finds it hardest to ask for help—and to accept it. Accepting help implies vulnerability. I suspect at our core, none of us really wants to be on the receiving end of help. Givers and helpers come from a position of power and strength; in expressing our needs, we inherently expose our weaknesses.

One woman, a widow for nearly a decade, shared this wisdom with me: "When people offer to help, say yes. And ask for help."

Ask for help. Three simple words that could have changed my miserable month.

Another woman said a neighbor shouted out across her lawn asking if he could help as she returned from her husband's burial. She immediately said, "Yes. Please mow my lawn." Before his death, her husband had purchased a John Deere riding lawn mower and had showed her how to use it. But she didn't want to use it. Her husband had always mowed the lawn and she didn't want to pick up this task. Her neighbor was thrilled to have access to the shiny new riding mower. He gladly used it to mow her lawn and his own. Nine years later, he still mows her lawn. That is a great example of "yes, thank you for your offer, here's what I need."

I have come to realize that not asking for help is not a sign of strength, but rather a sign of my own pride and weakness. My failure to disclose my needs to those I love only isolated me. My actions did not lead to being a more fully integrated part of my community. Instead, I acted as if I was only worthy if I had something to offer. When I was in need, I put myself on the proverbial ice floe.

Habit of resilience

ASK FOR HELP

Sometimes resilient people look so much more capable than we are; they seem to bounce back more quickly and they don't seem to need all the support we do in our grief journey. But they don't do it alone. Resilient people are much more likely to have strong social connections—they are not lone wolves. Thinking we can muscle through our pain alone or wait until someone offers unsolicited help often creates a cycle of isolation, resentment, and self-pity.

Asking for help is not easy. But if we believe in the unity of the body of Christ as Paul describes in Corinthians, then each one of us is a crucial yet incomplete part of a whole. If some are ears and some are eyes, none of us can function completely without the other. When we fail to ask for help that we so clearly need, we act out of arrogance and ignorance. We act as if we are whole and complete within ourselves. But as Paul reminds us: "To each one the manifestation of the Spirit is given for the common good" (1 Corinthians 12:7).

Asking for help is not a sign of weakness. It is an awareness of our own limitations and our profound interconnectedness. It is an awareness that our gifts were given to us for the common good.

REFLECTION

Sometimes others have an easier time noticing what we are good at and can help us name our true gifts. Can you name three of your gifts? Are there people in your life who know you well enough to help you identify your gifts?

When facing tough times, what would your best self ask of you and of others?

Accepting grief in the new normal

❧ 9 ❧

RESILIENCE IN LIMINAL SPACE

My son Thomas was due one month before my thirtieth birthday. You'd think that I would have been better prepared, but I was clueless. My husband and I, fearing we were infertile, had spent too much time fretting over whether we could ever become parents. When we finally conceived, we acted like this was the difficult part of parenting. Objectively, this part wasn't as easy for us as for many. But now that I've raised teenagers, even I recognize that conception is one of the sweeter parenting tasks.

Thomas was born in Scottsdale, Arizona. At the time, both of our families lived in Connecticut, either a two- or three-hour time zone change away, depending on the season. Arizona does not observe Daylight Saving Time, a detail my mother never fully grasped. At 5 AM, the phone would ring: Mom was calling so she could catch me before work.

These early morning calls were little solace and only served as a jarring reminder of my isolation. I had a colicky baby born in the middle of the summer heat on a 115-degree day, and my closest family was a three-hour flight away. Isolation wasn't my only hurdle. My maternal ineptitude was apparently glaringly obvious; the nurses took me aside before Thomas and I were discharged to teach me how to bathe my newborn. It was that bad.

A colleague called when I had been home for two weeks with my newborn and asked what I was doing with all my free time. I hesitated telling her the unvarnished truth: I could barely get my teeth brushed before noon, and I considered the day a success if I showered. Her casual question felt like a recrimination and confirmation that I was in fact the least competent mom on the planet.

One evening around dusk when Thomas was three months old, the doorbell rang. My husband was traveling and so I peeked through a side window and discovered a pack of miniature superheroes. It was Halloween, and I'd completely missed it. How had I not noticed the obvious displays of candy in the grocery store? Did the concept of a calendar even exist in my world anymore?

I was stumbling bleary-eyed into my new normal, and doing it poorly. I moved through each day in survival mode. A successful day involved basic grooming—a shower and a toothbrush. As one friend put it, we all have our standards. Mine just happened to be very low.

This is what lurching into "the new normal" looks like. Finding our feet when the rug has been pulled out isn't easy or pretty. I desperately wanted a child. Everything about Thomas was a blessing in my life, and finding my new normal was still one ugly transition. Imagine how much more difficult it can get when the dramatic change in your life isn't something you've dreamed of and hoped for. Imagine if the love of your life dies, and you find yourself washed up on an unfamiliar shore.

Sometimes we get stuck. In our fear, sleep deprivation, or overwhelming anxiety, we believe this rocky transition is our new normal. It is not. The rocky time is the liminal space between our old life and our new normal.

In Roman mythology, Janus was portrayed with one face looking forward and one backward. Teetering between the new year and the old, he was the god of doors, beginnings, and sunsets and sunrises.

How do we navigate an interval, or what theologians call *liminal* space? Being at the threshold between an ending and a beginning calls for a unique way of being. It's easy to spend too much time evaluating and perhaps regretting what just happened, or being worried about what's next. We don't know how long the transition will take, and in our fear of the unknown, we may be tempted to kick open the nearest door, anything to flee what Richard Rohr describes as "this terrible cloud of unknowing."[1]

Rohr talks about training to hold anxiety, to live with ambiguity, and to entrust and wait to see where God is leading us. To hold anxiety and ambiguity, we need faith and trust in ourselves and in the potential guides around us. We need a discipline of prayer, meditation, or exercise to sustain us in the unknowing of the transition. We need the willingness to let go of regrets and resentments about what is ending, and acceptance of taking up the new.

Jeffrey McDaniel writes, "I realize there's something incredibly honest about trees in winter, how they're experts at letting things go."[2]

This is liminal space, the in-between times in our lives when we have shed one skin and not yet grown fully into the next. We wait, like the tree, no longer in the glorious splendor of fall color, and not yet in the riotous emergence of spring green.

---

1   Richard Rohr, "Grieving as Sacred Space," *Sojourners*, January-February 2002. Found 8/29/2014 at http://sojo.net/magazine/2002/01/grieving-sacred-space.

2   Jeffrey McDaniel, found 8/30/14 at http://www.sparkpeople.com/mypage_public_journal_individual.asp?blog_id=5450506.

Most of us dread the winter times in our lives, the barren days of not knowing. We want to step out of one stage of our lives and immediately into the next, forgetting that new growth can't emerge unless the leaves first fall. We want doors to open for us before we close the doors behind us.

But liminal space is the chrysalis in our lives: the time we are neither caterpillar nor butterfly. It is difficult to embrace the cocoon times in our lives. The cocoon can be a dark and fearful place, a time of unknowing. Even if we hope it is a space where transformation can happen, it often doesn't feel transformative in the moment. It feels like fear and darkness.

Perhaps this is what grief feels like for you now, a space so dark you cannot even see the threshold. It may feel like empty solace to be told that transformation will happen, but it will. Knowing that the sunrise will come, we all begin to perceive the outlines of the new place where we will find ourselves on the other side of the threshold.

Habit of resilience

EMBRACE AMBIGUITY

Embracing anything in the dark days of grief is asking a lot. Perhaps you can only tolerate ambiguity right now. If so, consider it a victory.

Ambiguity is difficult. We want our lives ordered and predictable. We want to know what comes next, to see the threshold and know what is on the other side. But grief is not easily tamed. It is rarely predictable. It is never likable. We'd like to stomp our way right over the threshold into light. But grief makes us grope in the dark, trying to find our way out. Know that this is part of grief, a part you won't like.

Reflection

Do you sometimes ask yourself, "Who am I now?"

Looking back over your grief journey, what helped you recognize that you were moving forward?

❧ 10 ❧

RESILIENCE THROUGH GRIEF ATTACKS

In her book *The Year of Magical Thinking*, Joan Didion shares a story of hanging on to her husband's shoes so he might wear them when he returns. Except her husband is dead. Welcome to the crazy-making world of grief. We know our loved one is dead, yet we still find ourselves doing completely nonsensical things like keeping their shoes by the door just in case.

Occasionally when I am driving, I'll think, "I should call Mom." It's a fleeting thought, usually sparked by a riotously blooming garden. But there it is, "I should call Mom." Only Mom's been dead for over a year, and she had dementia for years before that. It's been years since I could casually pick up the phone to have a conversation with Mom. I know she is gone, but I suspect the bigger reality is this: my connection to Mom is not gone.

The people we love may be gone from our sight, but we are still firmly tethered to them. Who we are and who we've become is often indelibly linked to our beloved, and death does not change that. We are still in relationship with our deceased loved ones. And as people of faith, we talk across the grave all the time.

If saving shoes is one of grief's gentler crazy-making moments, grief attacks are full throttle ambushes. One of the hallmarks of a grief attack is its suddenness: with no warning, we become a blubbering mess. A tidal wave of grief flattens us, pounding us into the sand at the bottom of the ocean. This wave of grief owns us and there is nothing we can do until we get washed up on shore again, depleted and exhausted.

Grief attacks are terribly distressing. It's not an anniversary or a birthday; we aren't standing at the gravesite where we expect to be emotional. Grief attacks happen in our everyday living in unexpected ways. And they make us feel crazy and out of control.

Almost everyone who has experienced deep grief has experienced a grief attack. They often happen on ordinary days doing mundane things. Here are two examples:

Sally was grocery shopping when she spied her husband's favorite cereal. Right there in the cereal aisle, she lost it. She hadn't expected a box of cereal to take her over the edge. Embarrassed by her tears, she abandoned her cart and fled the store.

Fred was walking into church when he inhaled a whiff of his wife's favorite fragrance. Unable to hold it together emotionally, he kept walking right out of the building by a far exit. He walked around the building the long way until the pews were filled and he felt confident he could get to his car in the parking lot without encountering anyone.

Grief attacks sound pretty awful, and for most people they are. This is why people try to avoid a grief attack at all costs. But there's a catch: we *can't* avoid them. They arrive unannounced and completely out of the blue whether we've diligently avoided every favorite restaurant or overly familiar hospital floor, or disposed of every shred of our beloved's clothing. We feel crazy, but we're not. We're grieving.

The good news is that grief attacks for most people get less and less frequent and arrive with less intensity over time. In the meantime, carry Kleenex.

Habit of resilience

ACCEPT GRIEF ATTACKS AS A NORMAL PART OF GRIEVING

If a grief attack feels like a full-body slam, who in their right mind would want to accept one? But really, what choice do we have? Grief attacks don't ask for our permission to come visit. They show up wanted or not.

Accepting them as "normal" does help. Grief has a way of throwing us off balance. Too often, we think we are swimming in the deep end of the ocean of grief. Grief can be so disorienting that it is hard to believe our experience is "normal." But it is.

Now, knowing that our out-of-control feelings are normal is puny solace. I'll grant you that.

If you are feeling overwhelmed by grief, try this exercise. Imagine your grief is an object. Pick it up and place it in a trunk. Close the trunk lid and padlock the trunk shut. Decide how long you will keep the trunk locked—twenty minutes, an entire day? Practice setting your grief aside briefly each day for a short island of respite.

REFLECTION

Complete the sentence: "I am most embarrassed by my grief when

_____."

When you have a grief attack, what do you do to feel better?

❈ 11 ❈

RESILIENCE DURING
THE HOLIDAYS:
THE EMPTY CHAIR

When I was a child growing up in New England, our town had a small patch of ground encircled by many of the town's churches. It was called God's Acre. Each Christmas Eve, families would celebrate in their own church, and afterwards the entire town would spill out onto God's Acre to sing Christmas carols. Staunch traditionalists sang by the flickering glow of candlelight; pragmatists used flashlights. All of us huddled around tiny lights: friends, families, and neighbors.

Every year, our church service repeated every past Christmas Eve service, with the same songs, readings, and message, even the same vocalists. With the exception of the prominently displayed year on the song sheets, nothing else changed. Not a word. We really didn't need the song sheets since we knew every carol by heart. The candle required finesse. You had to hold it in a way that it cast light on the portion of the page you were singing, and use the page for some modicum of wind protection. But you couldn't get the page too close, lest you burned your song sheet. Candle wax was another issue, usually coating the mittened hand of the holder. These things never changed; the only thing that seemed to change was how fast we sang. This was entirely dependent on the weather. If it was bitter cold, the brass band played with unusual speed and vigor. The last song, "Joy to the World," often sounded like an express train accelerating into the frosty night.

Holidays are freighted with plenty of meaning and tradition. The scent of evergreen and delicious smells wafting from the kitchen on holidays evokes memories. As much as we joke about the unchanging nature of church services, our traditions ground us. Change, it seems, especially at the holidays, is an unwelcome guest.

When it became clear we were about to celebrate my father-in-law's last Christmas, we all gathered at the farm. Even before Christmas came, the holiday had taken on special meaning; it would be our last with Mike, our last time around the table for the Christmas feast, our last time opening presents together Christmas morning.

When Christmas dinner arrived, we had braced ourselves for the last time Mike would be with us at the table. But he wasn't. He felt too ill to join us for dinner, so there was his empty chair, sooner than we'd hoped for or expected.

The empty chair spoke volumes. Like most families, each of us had a particular chair at the table. Mike's was a commanding wingback chair that sat at the head of the table. We were all sad and shaken by the news that Mike was too ill to join us, but none more than my mother-in-law, who looked at the chair, turned to my husband, and said, "Steve, will you please take the head of the table?" And in that moment, we began a transition that none of us wanted or were ready to embrace. As we feared, Mike died two months later.

One widow shared with me that every year her family gathered at their cabin. Her husband, a morning person by nature, would get up early to make a huge pancake breakfast. When sleepy-eyed kids and grandkids would emerge, he would belt out a rendition of a children's song that began "Good morning to you, good morning to you, you look rather sleepy, in fact you look creepy." The silliness of the song, the pancakes, and their grandfather's bellowing voice were all part of being at the cabin as family. She knew that this year's morning silence would be haunting; the very walls of the cabin would be groaning, "Life has changed."

The empty chair, the person missing from our family portrait, the silence at breakfast—these are all things that bring out a deep sadness and longing.

Too often, we as family experience these events but do not express our sadness openly. We all sit at the breakfast table thinking of Grandpa's crazy song, but no one says a word. We eat in silence, pancakes tasting like cardboard, fearing that if we mention our sadness it will remind someone else of the song and make them sad.

Fear not! Everyone in the room is probably thinking the same thing. Everyone is trying to swallow their grief, one bite at a time. Sometimes, the most healing option is to name the sadness in the room, to say out loud that you are missing hearing Grandpa's crazy song. Usually when one person names their sadness, the room erupts with other funny Grandpa stories, and the family laughs and cries through breakfast deciding whether they will take up the mantle of collectively belting out the song in Grandpa's memory, or adopt a new tradition.

Holidays and family times take on new meanings when we've lost a loved one through death. With some thought and care, holidays can become *holy* days, times of remembrance with stories and celebration.

When we are at the farm on a holiday, particularly Father's Day or Memorial Day, we often hike out to Mike's grave. The family plot is part of a pioneer cemetery that sits on a small hillock a few hundred yards from the farmhouse. Unlike the day of his burial, when we solemnly walked in procession in jackets, suits, and funeral attire, these impromptu gravesite visits are always a ragtag band of family in jeans and fleeces, with dogs running beside us, all of us dodging cow pies as we hike across the fields to gather around Mike's grave. We usually sing a song and say the Our Father. It is a simple time to remember Mike as a family.

Habit of resilience

NAME THE SADNESS

"Give sorrow words. The grief that does not speak whispers the o'er-fraught heart, and bids it break." MACBETH—ACT IV, SCENE 3

Nearly every mourner seems to agree on this: they want others to remember their loved one by name. Talking about our grief helps. Naming our loved one helps. Saying what everyone is thinking is not only all right, it helps. If you are staring at your pancakes thinking, "I miss Grandpa," say it. Name the sadness. As Susan Gilbert Dickinson wrote to her sister-in-law Emily in 1861, "If a nightingale sings with her breast against a thorn, why not we?"

REFLECTION

As you think about the holidays, what traditions have changed since the death of your loved one? How have you incorporated their memory into your new traditions?

Birthdays and anniversaries, including the anniversary of the date of death, are often particularly difficult days. You remember, but often the world has moved on and does not remember or mark these days as significant. How have you turned these days into holy days of remembrance?

✺ 12 ✺

Resilience in caregiving

For everything there is a season, and a time for
every matter under heaven. ECCLESIASTES 3:1

When Kate's husband Bill died of cancer, she felt a sense of relief, then guilt. She had been his constant companion and caregiver for nearly five years. In the early years, she accompanied him to his doctor appointments in solidarity; they would go through this illness together. In the later years, she accompanied him out of practicality; he was no longer physically able to transport himself. He could still plod along, but the strength needed to fold up the walker, place it in the backseat of their car, and maneuver into the driver's seat was beyond him.

Others offered to help, but Bill wanted Kate with him, and Kate abided by his wishes. As much as she longed for even the briefest respite, she could not tell him the truth—she would be glad to have someone else help with the endless doctor visits. Treatment options had narrowed, and his doctors suggested Bill consider the addition of palliative care, care focused on his physical, emotional, and spiritual comfort.

At first, Bill had balked, thinking palliative care was the equivalent of hospice, and that hospice was the equivalent of throwing in the towel. But his doctor assured Bill he could receive treatment as well as palliative care. One week with the palliative care team, and Bill was sold. He slept better after the palliative care team adjusted his meds—not in quantity or dose; they simply tweaked the time of day he took them. The palliative care team seemed to have more time to talk to Bill, asking what he wanted, pushing beyond the simple answer of "I want to get better." What else did he hope for?

Kate was grateful for the added support. The palliative care team engaged Bill in thoughtful questions, things she wanted to discuss but was hesitant to bring up. Frankly, she'd been so tired, overwhelmed, and focused on ridding Bill of cancer that she hadn't had time to ask the bigger questions. What did he hope for in the coming months? How did he want to spend his time? The palliative care team gave Bill permission to think about the time he had left, an unknown variable that looked more like days and months, not years.

Kate faced a different struggle. For years, she'd helped Bill battle cancer. Battle was the best word she could use because that's what it felt like—a constant onslaught from an unrelenting disease. Now she was faced with a different challenge: saying goodbye, and facing a new and unbidden life as a widow.

So much of Kate's life had been on hold for the last five years. Friends had been pushed off. Kate couldn't remember the last time she'd been to her favorite yoga class or read a book. Cancer had not only taken over Bill's body; it had commandeered her calendar as well.

Kate and Bill's kids were close to their parents, but not close by. Their daughter had married a year ago; Kate had suspected the wedding had been pushed forward to make sure Bill was still on earth, although her daughter never admitted this. Her daughter and her new husband checked in weekly by phone. Kate had discouraged Skype because it was too difficult to manage the image that all was well when Bill's increasingly moon-shaped face betrayed the volume of steroids he was taking. His round, puffy face did not look like the chisel-cut, handsome face of the man she married, nor did it look like the dad who had walked their daughter down the aisle one year ago.

Their son was closer, five hours by car and in grad school. He seemed more aware of the progression of Bill's illness, but the words "How can I help?" never came out of his mouth. Kate bore the day-to-day tasks of feeding, bathing, and medication management. Kate was conflicted; part of her felt Bill's illness should be her burden, not her kids'. Another part longed for someone to help shoulder the load. What began as a partnership to tackle Bill's illness was dissolving. Bill was unable to care for himself, much less any of the routine household tasks. Kate felt she had to carry the load for both of them, shouldering not only Bill's care, but all the other day-to-day needs.

Near the end, when Bill had days and possibly weeks, Kate felt physically and emotionally spent. Although she felt guilty for even thinking this, a part of her was relieved this would soon be over; if Bill was at all alert, he was suffering. Friends who had once come over for lively dinners now stopped by for what Kate called "pity calls," short visits that usually ended with some version of pep-rally cheerleading to encourage Bill to "hang in there" or "give it all you've got." Kate had thought friends rallying around her would help, but they only made her feel worse. No one seemed to be willing to talk about the obvious, that Bill was dying. Friends who Kate knew would never see Bill alive again left the house with a chipper, "See you soon," when it was obvious that the next time they would see Bill was when he would be in a casket.

Kate felt guilty about her first thoughts after Bill's death. She could get a good night's sleep again and she could cook. (Cooking, her passion, had nauseated Bill. What smelled so welcoming and delicious to her sent him into agony.) The pleasures of cooking and sleep sounded so trivial to her, because her husband was dead. Yet there they were, thoughts that felt so trivial, disloyal, and selfish. She hated herself for feeling grateful to have her life back. She hated that Bill was not there to share her new life with her.

A few weeks after Bill's funeral, Kate ran into an acquaintance in a clothing store. The woman acknowledged Kate's loss and then made some sputtering remark about being surprised to see Kate out and enjoying herself so soon. Kate said she wanted to slap her. "This woman didn't have a clue," she said, clearly getting heated up just remembering the encounter. "I'd lost fifteen pounds in those years; everything I owned hung on me like a hand-me-down. I have no doubt this woman had shopped for clothes dozens of times in the five years I spent cleaning up vomit." Kate was steamed. The idea that this woman thought Kate should be cloistered in mourning made her even madder.

Kate ranted a bit longer about this doltish woman. "Five years, five years, what more does she want?" Kate repeated. Then she stopped, took a deep breath, and started laughing. It was an epiphany. She felt judged by this woman who had made her feel she was being disloyal to Bill by enjoying a small part of life again so soon. Kate realized conflicting emotions were normal and that her sadness and her relief were both authentic parts of her grief process; she couldn't block out one emotion without blocking out all emotions.

Of course she was sad! Of course she missed Bill; but five years of caregiving had left her with a firm determination to live her life as fully as possible. Cloistering herself in her home in grief felt inauthentic, as if she was trying to prove to the world how much she loved Bill. She knew in that moment of much-needed laughter that cloistering herself didn't serve her well; she had nothing to prove, especially to random acquaintances. Bill's illness was witness enough of how fleeting and precious life is.

Her anger had softened and she said, "I'm glad I ran into her. That flash of anger helped me sort all these mixed-up, conflicting feelings. I knew I felt guilty, I just didn't know why. Bill would have been pleased to see me shop. He more than anyone would want to see me living vibrantly again. She made me so mad, but it turns out she gave me a gift."

Habit of resilience

GIVE YOURSELF PERMISSION TO MOVE ON

The greatest gift we can give our loved ones is to live our lives fully. When you feel ready to move on, do it. Without guilt. Your loved one would heartily approve.

REFLECTION

Does it ever feel disloyal to your loved one to enjoy life again? Have you given yourself permission to enjoy life again, to smile or even laugh?

Grief almost always serves up conflicted feelings. Sadness, guilt, and relief are sometimes bundled together. Can you name conflicted feelings you have felt?

❦ 13 ❦

RESILIENCE: SORTING THROUGH THE STUFF

If we're lucky, we are blessed with an overabundance of something. I have a pack of fabulous aunts on all sides, not just on my mother's and father's side, but on my husband's side too. Each one of them served as a role model for me of what I might become as an adult woman, a mother, an aunt, or a wife. I loved visiting with them, hearing about their lives, and letting them love me, as aunts are prone to do. Of course, most of them did not know each other, nor did they know, I suspect, how much they influenced my life.

My husband comes from a surprisingly small family. I've often joked that he had one of everything he needed: one mother, one father, one sibling, one cousin, one aunt, and one uncle.

Steve's Aunt Nancy was my mother-in-law's sister, and she was a hoot. She was direct, funny, irreverent, and opinionated, and I adored her. Talking to her was like being invited into a secret girls club, where someone from your mother's generation told you the straight, unadulterated scoop, things you always suspected they believed but were too proper to say in public. Nancy had no qualms about speaking her truth in public, even if it made others uncomfortable. In fact, I think she enjoyed watching others squirm at hearing her unvarnished truth about a situation.

When Nancy's grandson turned sixteen, she took him on a road trip from Missouri to Savannah, Georgia, to explore the surroundings written about in the best-selling novel *Midnight in the Garden of Good and Evil.* More precisely, Bradley took *her*—a sixteen-year-old new driver, driving his grandmother in a convertible cross-country. Bradley was obsessed with the book, and Nancy was willing to indulge his literary curiosity. This did not surprise any of us: she was a librarian by profession, and she read voraciously.

The road trip seemed crazy to most of her friends, and I might add to some of her family, but it was quintessential Nancy. She seemed more than willing to point the car east and let the adventure unfold.

Some people seem to have the capacity to live life fully without concern for any behind-the-back tongue wagging about their life choices. Nancy was one of those people. She knew some people didn't approve of all of her choices, and she didn't care. She never asked to live their lives, and she had no intention of letting them live hers.

Nancy was in her seventies when her mother died at one hundred. A year later, we buried Nancy's husband. By this time, her brother-in-law (who was my father-in-law, Mike) was dealing with two primary cancers, and much of the family focus was around Mike's care and treatment plan.

By Mike's last Christmas, Nancy arrived at the farm tired and under treatment for pneumonia. The pneumonia had lingered for weeks, but the family's concern was on Mike's treatment and comfort, as he was clearly at the end of life. Two months later, Mike was dead.

Soon after Mike's funeral, attention shifted to Nancy's still lingering pneumonia. Nancy, like many women her age, had smoked as a younger woman, and she had been exposed to secondhand smoke much of her life. She had reasonable concerns about lung cancer, but had been told months earlier that she did not have cancer and did not need to worry about this.

Finally, in an attempt to understand her pneumonia, Nancy underwent a biopsy. Post op and before she was fully conscious, the family learned Nancy had a rare and aggressive form of lung cancer. She died eighteen days later.

Although Nancy had been ill for months, from the moment of her diagnosis until her death we felt as if we were on a freight train that no longer had brakes. An illness that had lingered for months now aggressively took hold. Six weeks after Mike's funeral, we buried Nancy. She was seventy-seven.

Nancy's death brought on a flood of grief reactions, and from the start it was clear that we were struggling with complicated grief, a situation that can occur when too many losses are layered on top of each other. Without enough time to process any one loss, each new loss triggers a reaction that is both about the most recent loss and often about the unresolved grief of older losses.

In the span of three years, my mother-in-law had lost her own mother, her brother-in-law, her sister and only sibling, and her husband. Everyone in her family from her generation was gone. What had started as a small family had gotten exponentially smaller. For Steve, his sister, and his cousin, each had lost a beloved grandmother, and Steve's cousin had lost both parents.

Nancy's death was complicated for other reasons as well; her illness had been in plain sight, and we had dismissed it, thinking a course of the right antibiotics would take care of her illness. We were laser focused on Mike's illness and easily lulled into the complacency of knowing Nancy's mother had lived to one hundred. We expected nothing less for Nancy.

Multiple deaths in a short time span are not the only situation that can trigger a more complicated grief response. Plenty of other issues can complicate our grief as well: suicide; murder; multiple deaths; violent death; shock of discovery; witnessing a death; when there is no body; when secrets are revealed after a death; when we had conflicted relationships with the deceased, unfinished business, or we were dependent on the deceased.

Infrequently, entire families collapse with emotion after a death, and one person stoically comes forward to lead. The leader holds the family together, plans the funeral, leads the burial, and tends to the dreaded legal aftermath. When the dust settles, the person who seemed so together at the outset may begin to grieve, only to discover her family has moved on in their grief. No longer emotionally fragile themselves, they wonder why she is suddenly such a sniffling mess. The super-responsible family member makes this painful discovery: keeping busy and overloaded with work will not prevent grief; it will only delay it, and, in some cases, prolong it.

Occasionally, people will have great difficulty coming home to a house filled with memories. Thinking they are processing their grief and moving on, they may prematurely sell their home. Moving on can actually be an attempt to move away from painful memories. But painful memories have a way of becoming precious. The memories churned up by a family home early in grief may feel raw and over-whelming at first. In time, they may bring comfort and peace, but once the house is gone, the memories and memorabilia associated with it are often no longer accessible.

Selling your home and moving to a new community with new neighbors, doctors, churches, grocery stores, and schools will keep you from bumping into painful memories. It will also keep you from potential circles of support. Often, a premature move prolongs grief.

Nancy's only son, John, did something brave and commendable. He did not immediately sell Nancy's house. Nancy lived in a small town, the same town she and her sister had grown up in. Her mother's home was a short walk from Nancy's house and had recently been sold. Nancy's home became the repository of family memories—childhood summers spent in this tiny town. The graves of John's grandparents and both parents were in this town. Nancy's life was tangible here: her books, her pineapple-etched glass windows, and closets filled with her husband's many silver-tipped canes. Every artifact spoke of her life.

After Nancy's burial, the family gathered on her screen porch. Suddenly, with little breeze, every wind chime on the porch started wildly chiming. Nancy was here with us, once again stirring things up and making a racket. It made us laugh.

Selling Nancy's house immediately might have seemed sensible to the world. After all, her son lived a couple of states away, and her sister and niece were both at least an hour from the house. There would be no family close by to watch or care for the house. But coming back to Nancy's house again and again gave us time to process our grief more fully, to touch and hold her things, to remember her and all she meant to us. Her house was our touchstone. The family had lived in this small town for seven decades, and now there was no one left, just Nancy's house and all of our memories.

Before John did sell Nancy's house, I dug up some of Nancy's vinca, a hardy groundcover. It has deep blue flowers, and every spring I am reminded that Nancy planted that very same vinca in her yard. I have another groundcover, pachysandra, from my mother's yard, and an oak tree transplanted as a weedy seedling growing at my parents' home. We have two large pine trees in the yard. They were saplings when we brought them home in washtubs from my husband's parents' farm. There are also iris and peonies and hosta, a yard full of memories and stories. When I step outside, I am surrounded by the very best memories of family, each one tending and nurturing a garden to create something of lasting beauty.

Habit of resilience

TAKE THE TIME YOU NEED

Grief has no timetable. The tradition of wearing black for a year in *Gone with the Wind* style has thankfully gone with the wind. I suspect that's because a year to grieve is too long for some and too short for others.

Grief falls more into the "Goldilocks and the Three Bears" model. We need to find our particular fit. Not too long, not too short, just right.

Well-intentioned people might encourage us to clean out our closets, sell the house, and move to another state. Slow down. Listen to your heart. What feels right for you? We don't grieve on a schedule. There are no right ways to grieve. Go at your own pace. You don't need to explain your choices to your kids, your in-laws, or your next-door neighbor. When your neighbor tells you she gave her husband's clothes to Goodwill the day of his funeral, smile as you are closing the door. Channel Aunt Nancy and then do what you want to do.

REFLECTION

Think of a tangible keepsake you kept as a memory of your loved one. What is it, and why does it bring back such warm memories?

Have you had an experience—like the wild ringing of the wind chimes—of your loved one visiting? Sometimes we shy away from sharing these stories for fear that people will politely nod but secretly think we are completely nuts. Are you hesitant to share your other-worldly experiences of your loved ones with others?

Speaking
to grief

✺ 14 ✺

HELPING OTHERS TO BECOME RESILIENT

The summer of 2014 left great swaths of the Southwest bone dry. Hot, dry conditions meant wild fires throughout California, and other southwest states were at constant risk. Fourth of July fireworks were banned in many southwestern cities, including Albuquerque, New Mexico. The threat of sparking a new wildfire was too great. But on the Fourth of July, there was one spectacular, albeit illegal, fireworks display. The Buddhist temple in town dazzled Albuquerque with the only local display. When charged with setting off fireworks illegally, the monks of the Buddhist temple claimed they do not read newspapers, do not listen to the radio, do not watch TV, and were unaware of the ban on fireworks. They discovered ignorance is not innocence.

Too many well-intentioned people pick the path of ignorance when it comes to choosing consoling words. Occasionally, people tell me they plan to dodge a wake or funeral altogether because "I just don't know what to say." I suspect not knowing what to say is only part of the discomfort. We don't like how death makes us feel, and we'd prefer squashing all the questions and fears about death that bubble up in our subconscious.

Even the most fervent Christian wonders, "Is this it? Will I ever see this person again?" The rawness of grief often challenges our neatly prepackaged beliefs, unravels accepted truths, and forces us to reexamine the very bedrock of our faith in an effort to claim something authentic and true for ourselves. Like a rewoven fabric, when we gather the threads of doubt and reweave our beliefs, we often end up with a stronger garment.

Some of the things we say at wakes and funerals may make us feel better and keep the howling, scary questions at bay. But do they make the bereaved feel better? When we utter something like "He is in a better place," do we say it for the bereaved or for ourselves? Do our words echo as recrimination instead of consolation for someone wondering if they will ever see their loved one again?

Jean was forty-nine when her husband died. It was a shock beyond words. Their kids were in college, and Jean was just opening her own store. Jean and her husband had spent the day attaching hooks and putting up fixtures in the dressing rooms of her new shop the day he died. That evening, at the wedding reception of a friend's daughter, Jean turned to ask her husband to dance. She thought he was next to her, but when she turned, he was gone. At first she imagined he'd slipped off to the bathroom; then she realized he was on the floor. He'd had a massive heart attack.

Jean knows her husband got the best care available; the bride's father was the town's fire chief. All the possible lifesaving measures were available immediately, yet Warren never regained consciousness. When they arrived at the hospital, Warren was pronounced dead. Jean recalls the chaplain, a Catholic sister, who repeatedly barked at her, "You're just going to have to face the fact. Your husband is dead."

That was thirty years ago. Jean laughs now and says, "If I'd had my wits about me, I would have decked her." The Catholic sister is probably long dead herself, but her words are not. Her callous remarks failed to consider Jean's situation. Just minutes before, Jean had been on the dance floor; now her husband was dead. When faced with such sudden and unexpected news, it is not uncommon to go into a state of shock. The initial numbness can serve as a protective barrier. We can only take in so much. Taking in the enormity of this life change doesn't happen faster if someone repeatedly demands we "face the facts."

Many of us often stumble our way through our condolences, not knowing what to say. People who have had loss in their own lives may be the most capable at finding the right words of condolence, although this is not always true. Once, in the hospital, I overheard a grief-stricken dad being verbally accosted by an unknown visitor. The visitor said, "One child, you only lost one child? Well, I lost both my children."

When expressing condolences, your primary job is to *listen*. Let the bereaved tell their story. If you find yourself tempted to tell a newly grieving person your tale of woe from years past, please, please, please, find more appropriate support for you. Join a grief group, find a compassionate listener—anything but burdening the newly bereaved with your still unresolved pain. Don't ask the newly bereaved to muster the energy to hear your painful story too.

Earlier this spring, a friend's son suicided[1] after years of struggling with depression and anxiety. He was seventeen. His high school re-

---

1   Some experts in the field of suicide awareness prefer the term "suicided" to "committed suicide." They believe that the word "committed" conjures negative associations. Suicide is the result of a brain disease, often an unsuccessfully treated depression. I use the term "suicided" in deference to their wisdom and experience.

sponded by asking people to send his parents a condolence card so his parents might receive a card a week for a year. My friend appreciated the gesture, yet she mentioned the cards only because she had received one that week that read "We will never know why God called your son home." My friend said, "God did not call my son home. God did not ask my son to hang himself. When he hanged himself, God welcomed him. But suicide was the result of his illness, not God calling!"

When a young person dies, either by illness, accident, or suicide, consoling words are especially difficult. It's hard to find the right words when everything about the situation seems wrong.

Phrases like "God only takes the good ones" or "God needed another rosebud for his garden" should be banished from our vocabularies.

Ditto for variations like "God needed another angel." If you are tempted to invoke God as the bad actor who willed someone's death, please don't. "You're young, you can have another child" implies children and babies are interchangeable Lego blocks, not miraculous, irreplaceable, and unique individuals.

God does not give us cancer so we learn some cosmic lesson. God does not snatch our babies in crib death or burden our precious children with terminal heart disease because the heavenly gardens are getting drab. All sorts of things happen in life. Some are terrible luck or bad timing, and some are outright horrifying and tragic. Believing God could have prevented all this bad stuff from happening and yet knowing bad stuff continues to happen brings us to one of the fundamental questions of faith. Why do people continue to get cancer, toddlers get run over accidently as their parents back out of their driveways, and people die of salmonella from eating cantaloupe? Where is God in all of this?

If God could have prevented our loved one's cancer or our friend's bike accident, why didn't God? Where is God in our misery and pain? I suspect the same place God was when Jesus was crucified, weeping with us at the foot of the cross, reminding us as the psalmist does so eloquently that God remembers us, God will never leave us, and God will be with us in our agony.

Some may feel abandoned by God's inaction. We seem infinitely more prone to shake our fist at God in our time of distress, bellowing "Where were you?" and less likely to kneel down next to a crocus miraculously emerging amidst a snowy spring and say, "Ah, there you are."

At a loss for words? "I'm sorry" goes a long way. A hug does too. We think words are necessary, but in bereavement, they are often optional. Your loving presence often says it all, and it's the most important gift you can give.

Say something loving about the deceased; add a personal story. What did you admire about the person; where did their gifts shine most brightly? How about "Your husband/wife/daughter/son was a really good person. I always admired the way he/she took time for people"? People like to know that you noticed and appreciated the best qualities of their loved one. Giving a concrete example of some lovable, caring, or competent trait is often much more comforting than platitudes. Actually, almost anything is more comforting than platitudes.

Habit of resilience

BE PRESENT EVEN WHEN TONGUE-TIED

Your presence matters more than your words. A hug is worth more than most sonnets. It's easier than you think. Just show up.

REFLECTION

Are there things people said to you that felt hurtful or insensitive? Realizing that they were doing their best to comfort you, can you forgive them?

When a friend comes to you for help about what to say to a newly bereaved, what is your best advice?

✣ 15 ✣

FINDING RESILIENCE
IN WRITING

When did I become old enough to have decades-long friendships? Somehow it happened. I got older, and some of my friends came along for the ride. And vice versa. Bob is one of those people. When we met, Bob was a young lawyer in need of an apartment. He was moving to New York City just as Steve and I were to be married. Steve's roommate, Jon, was a classmate of Bob's in law school. New York City rents being what they are, Jon was looking to fill the back bedroom. As quickly as Steve moved out, Bob moved in.

Bob and Jon quickly became Bob and Sharon and Jon and Sarah. Our twenty-something lives were full: new jobs, weddings, babies, and baptisms. We lived a less glamorous version of *Friends*. Death wasn't part of the mix.

When Bob's brother Frank died, his death was a first of sorts. Sure, we'd all buried grandparents and parents and aunts and uncles by then. But Frank was the first sibling to die, the first of our generation, and it felt entirely too close to the bone. Frank died suddenly of an aortic dissection. As Bob said, "Think of it as an aneurysm, only slower and more excruciating." His death felt completely out of season, too soon for even those of us who only knew him through the decades of Bob's storytelling.

Frank's daughter Shannon was twenty when he died. She was still in college and surrounded by other twenty-somethings who knew little about grief and loss. A gifted writer, Shannon began writing letters to her dad as a way to process her grief. With Shannon's permission, Bob forwarded her blog link. I read and wept and then asked if I might share a few of her letters with you. She graciously agreed.

Letter one

Dear Dad,

It's approaching 5 am in Toronto, and a nasty case of grief and heartburn is keeping me awake. I'm not sure which one is causing more tossing and turning.

You wrote me so many letters over the past twenty-two years and seven weeks. My favorite was the one you gave me on Father's Day: "100 Reasons I Love Being Your Dad." (I bought you a humor book on Rednecks that year, but I think you loved it just as much as I loved that letter.) I've misplaced the letter, but I know you saved everything you wrote. I don't think I ever returned a single letter, although I did call frequently. Very often your letters were too profound for me to process and reciprocate, but I will try my best here. Sometimes I talk to you late at night, but not long after I croak "I miss you," I start to feel a little crazy. Somehow blogging feels more normal. You were also the only person to check this blog every day while I was abroad, waiting to read, as you described it, "The World According to Shannon."

I aced my French oral exam last week, and Mom said that I earned that trip to France you two had planned. Back in June, while we were at Khwai Camp, you and Mom were agitated that I wanted to tag along on your trip to Paris next year (although my conversing with French guests made a good case). I hadn't considered that that trip was supposed to be another honeymoon. The day after you died, within ten minutes of seeing Mom, she asked me if I would take her to Paris. I promise to take good care of her—lots of good food, wine, shopping, and no museum death marches…

The hardest part of all of this is that all of my expectations have proved to be wrong. Mom and I have learned that we can't will ourselves through this. I think we're doing everything we're supposed to do—exercising, eating, sleeping (most of the time), socializing, crying when needed.… Running has helped. My injuries are under control, so hopefully I will be able to start a real build-up after the New Year. As I'm sure you know from when your parents died—and I know how much that haunted you—there is no total escape, only time.

I miss you every day. Some days I wake up and things seem normal, and only after my second cup of coffee am I sucker-punched by the grief. Other days, your absence is a constant, paralyzing, presence. I am told that this will fade. I'm not sure if I want it to, because you deserve every ounce of misery I feel for your loss.

I love you, Dad, and I promise to carry you with me forever.

— Shannon Joy

Letter two

Dear Dad,

The past few days have been rough. I don't know why. Of course I know, but there's no trigger for me to control. A cloud appears in a valley with no wind to carry it away.

I'm going home next week to help Mom move. She's continuing with the renovation. The house needs it. She needs it. But I can't stand the thought of not being able to crawl into the green chair in your office, where I would watch you neatly put together the pieces of life's puzzles.

The tears would disappear. A dog would sleep by the window, knowing that your office was the place where decisions were made and laughter was created. I hope that chair won't become lost in the keep/give away/ throw away mess.

Yesterday, a professor called me out publicly for not participating in a seminar. You of all people would know that this was out of character for me; I have my opinions and I'm proud of them. I haven't told any of my professors what I'm dealing with, but I may have to. The awful days are less frequent, but they're no less taxing. I'm thankful that I can—not coincidentally—slink into my chair in a lecture hall for most of my classes this semester, but this one requires a level of engagement that will escape me from time to time, despite my interest in the course itself.

I didn't tell her that it took all my energy to complete the readings over the weekend, to come prepared to class, to come to class at all. By the time I could wrap my head around the readings, the questions posed, and the (few) relevant responses of my classmates, we had long moved on. I was so damn mad. She grouped me together with the lazy kids in the back, who haven't even read the syllabus. Two dozen pairs of eager beaver eyes cut into me as if I'd said that human rights don't exist. It was just so hard to focus yesterday, and I didn't want to engage in a debate just for the sake of impressing people. You would have seen right through that kind of participation.

When does it become inappropriate to explain everything? When will your death become irrelevant?

I'm still doing everything I'm supposed to do. I ran really far and hard today, and my hip is paying for it. God, that lactic acid felt good.

I love you, Dad, and I promise to carry you with me forever.

—Shannon Joy

Dad's Turn

After another week of pretending that I can take a full course load, that my work at the paper is easy, and that neither a strained gluteus medius nor plantar fasciitis will impede training for the NYC half-marathon, I wanted to call home. I didn't want to call my mom, the only person who could conceivably pick up the phone. I rationalized (without really thinking at all) that I'd called my mom a lot recently, and it was Dad's turn to hear "the world according to Shannon."

But last night, for no particular reason, I wanted to call my dad. Not knowing how to process such a thought, I grabbed a blanket and went to sleep, fully clothed. I never expected grief to be so physically exhausting. The day was over; the hurt couldn't be undone.

When I woke up, I realized that my mom must feel like this way every day.

Letter five

Dear Dad,

It's been a year and a half. I'd lost track of the date, but saw it on my phone at 6:30 am. I had a running date with an old friend, a mentor really, and upon doing the math, I just wanted to hide under the covers. I've long stopped noticing the 28th of each month. The self-inflicted pain was pointless. Dakota dragged me out of bed, and out the door I went. I had to pound out the misery on pavement, for today we had a celebration. Eight miles would do.

I flew home for a baby shower. That's right. On top of everything else, you're missing out on being a grandparent. It was quite the party, with Alan catering and Mom doing everything just so. I met some truly awesome women—real pioneers and leaders in their field. The shower, of course, was about my soon-to-be niece, but my mind kept drifting. You always taught me to look for role models, to be gritty in my search for

*excellence. Between the oohs and aahs of opening presents, I tried to ask
these women as many questions as possible. You were my number one fan
and taught me to be a feminist. I can't replace you, but one day I might
have enough role models and mentors. Maybe.*

*I ran again tonight. So much has happened in the past eighteen
months, but when the bad days hit they're the same as ever. That pain in
my sternum that surfaces when I've held back one too many tears.*

*As I type, Mom is en route to give a speech in the morning. She's
going to speak about the impact of debate on her life. She gave me a
preview—and I assure you she will kill it tomorrow, as always—but
we both know that she left out debate's biggest impact on her life. I leave
early in the morning, so Dakota is being boarded. I have one night alone
in the house—this big, beautiful, renovated home—and it's just so
damn quiet. I miss everything, but mostly the chuckles.*

I love you, Dad, and I promise to carry you with me forever.

— Shannon Joy

Habit of resilience

JOURNAL

Writing has a way of clarifying your thinking. It is a safe outlet to say
things you aren't sure you are ready to say yet. When we want to pick
up the phone and check in with our loved one but we know we can't,
we can write.

Writing also gives us a retrospective on our grief. All of us have
moments when we feel absolutely stuck, as if we have not moved one
inch in our grief journey since the moment we first knew our loved
one was dead. But our journals tell us otherwise. When we reread our

journals, we realize we have made progress. We see it there in print. Journaling can give us the courage to keep going.

Reflection

What do you wish you had asked or said to your loved one? Could you write your loved one a letter and tell them now?

What special memories do you have that you most want to keep alive? Could you journal about these memories to capture the details that you most want to savor?

❧ 16 ❧

RESILIENCE IN GRIEF
WITHOUT WORDS:
YOUR SENSES AND GRIEF

Grief is a full-body experience. We expect it to be emotionally exhausting but we are sometimes surprised to find it physically draining as well. Grief sneaks up on us. We inhale a whiff of fragrant roses and we are flooded with memories. We save old voice mails, fearing we will forget the voice of our loved one. Just one bite of some foods is enough to conjure the memory of a special meal long ago. Our favorite photos have pride of place within our homes. Our loved ones may be gone from our sight, but their images are ever present. We may hold on to a flannel shirt or robe because the touch and smell evoke our loved one.

Maybe we expected grief to feel like emotional pain. But emotional pain is real pain. We can experience grief as a deep physical ache. Grief does not just exist as a concept in our heads. Grief is ever present. It is in all we see, taste, feel, hear, and smell.

Sometimes we think we can talk our way through grief. Helpful as they are, thinking and talking do not engage our whole body. Our words never fully capture the essence and depth of our pain. Sometimes there are no words for what we feel. We want to understand our grief in explainable ways, but it is not always possible. Grief can inhabit non-verbal spaces within us, places of ache so deep that our words seem shallow and hollow compared to our experience. Tapping into all of our senses can help us process grief more completely.

A friend mentioned that after 9/11, whenever he was in his car he listened to Leonard Bernstein's first recording of Mahler's Second Symphony or Eric Leinsdorf's recording of Verdi's *Requiem*. For months he toggled back and forth, symphony to requiem. In the music, he could encounter God. Music helped structure what was otherwise out-of-control grief.

Music touches deep emotion within us. For many, music is the most direct way God connects with us. My husband listens to the King's College Choir's Lessons and Carols on the radio every Christmas Eve. And every Christmas Eve, he cries when the first young voice begins "Once in Royal David's City." Don't ask him why he cries. He doesn't know. Don't ask us why we cry either. "I'm sad" is a completely insufficient response to something so much greater— but our words fail us. Not all tears have words.

Touch is another sense that grievers often hesitate to mention. Those who've lost a spouse may feel the loss of touch acutely, not simply the intimate contact couples enjoy but also someone to kiss you goodbye in the morning and hug you when you come home from work. After a coworker's husband died, a friend stopped by before work every morning for six weeks. She got out of her car, hugged my coworker, and said simply, "Have the best day you can." The daily hug made a difference and, sixteen years later, my coworker still remembers this kindness.

Pets ground us. Not only do they love us unconditionally, they keep us from grieving solely through our rearview mirror. A friend said, "Dogs and cats particularly, like children, help us to live in the present, which is a skill needed in the grieving process. And the present is the only place we meet God."

Habit of resilience

ENGAGE ALL YOUR SENSES IN GRIEF

Just as an unexpected scent can hurdle us into an unexpected grief attack, scent can also evoke warm memories our thoughts alone cannot fully capture. The smell of cologne, the softness of a favorite flannel shirt, or the voice on your voicemail may be too much to bear at first. But in time, each will bring its own precious memory. Listen to music that seems to resonate with your grief. Schedule massages if you are missing touch. Hold cherished objects in your hand. Let your senses tap into the unspoken parts of your grief. Let your tears flow without worrying where they came from and when they will stop. Someday you will sing and laugh again. Like some tears, your laughter will have no words. Embrace them both.

Engage all your senses in your grief journey. Play with clay; draw with crayons; play music that is healing; cook; take a warm bath. Get a dog. Let every fiber of your body cry out in grief.

Also, pray! Pray without words—try Centering Prayer. Centering Prayer is a silent prayer form that prepares us to receive God within us. Unlike most prayer, it is receptive prayer, intended to help us receive Christ within us. As a contemplative prayer form, it lets us rest in God, silencing our words and our thoughts to simply be with God.

Reflection

Where do you encounter God? In words and prayer, music and images?

What color is your grief today? If your grief were a food, what would it be? What music best captures your grief?

❧ 17 ❧

RESILIENCE IN FORGIVING OURSELVES

As the horrific drama of the shootings at Sandy Hook Elementary un-folded, Peter Lanza is reported to have noticed his colleagues gathered around the TV. Briefly noticing the name of the school, Peter com-mented that his sons had gone to that school, then he went back to his office. The early reports identified two potential shooters, a twen-ty- and twenty-four-year-old, exactly the ages of his sons. The CNN reporter also noted that both had attended Sandy Hook. As the eerie coincidences mounted, Peter left work to go home and listen to the news. Although he did not know it yet, his life had just changed forever.

By this time, CNN was identifying the shooter as Ryan Lanza, Peter's older son. Peter called his wife, Shelley. Peter says he knew Ryan was not involved; he also suspected Adam was the shooter. Peter and Shelley headed to Hoboken to be with Ryan. By the time they arrived, police had already escorted Ryan to the police station. By now, the news had confirmed twenty children and six adults at Sandy Hook Elementary school were dead. Also dead were Nancy Lanza, Adam's mother, and Adam, who had suicided. After hours of being questioned, Ryan, Peter, and Shelly, were escorted to Peter's aunt's home, the first of many safe houses.

In the early days, Ryan, Peter, and Shelley lived in liminal space; on the one hand, questioned by the FBI, the state police, and others; and on the other, offered police protection and a canine unit for their safety.

Peter Lanza considered changing his name, knowing that his name defined him before people even met him. He has commented that although his old friends have been unshakable, he is unsure if he will ever make new friends. The events of December 14, 2012, brought his life to a full stop.

As the first anniversary of the massacre approached, Peter broke his silence and approached Andrew Solomon, who wrote a piece for *The New Yorker* titled "The Reckoning."[2] Peter's purpose was to help prevent this from happening again. "I need to get some good from this," he said. "And there is no place else to find any good. If I could generate something to help them, it doesn't replace them, it doesn't—but I would trade places with them in a heartbeat if that would help."

After a year of storage in their attic, Peter and his wife Shelley finally opened "the stuff," the boxes of letters, crosses, teddy bears, even candy that had been sent to him since the massacre. Peter reportedly showed Andrew Solomon a bag of caramels, now a year old. He wouldn't eat them or allow anyone else to eat them, fearing they might be poisoned. Yet he couldn't bring himself to throw them away either. This is his painful dilemma—never knowing whether people are truly trying to support him in his grief or potentially trying to kill him.

---

2   Andrew Solomon, "The Reckoning," *The New Yorker*, March 17, 2014; accessed 9/1/14 at http://www.newyorker.com/magazine/2014/03/17/the-reckoning.

Peter Lanza lives in the between space now, never able to return to the uncomplicated life of pre-December 14, 2012, and struggling to emerge whole on the other side of this tragedy. He lives in the space between police questioning and police protection, between homemade caramels sent with heartfelt condolence and homemade caramels sent with poison.

Never knowing whom to trust, people like Peter Lanza often isolate themselves. They often do not feel they can fully claim what they have lost because others have lost so much more. Whom can they trust, whom can they cry with, and who will hear their gnashing of teeth and still love them?

Twenty-six families lost someone precious, a darling child or an adult who tried to protect the kids. I cannot imagine their loss, and I have often wondered if I would ever recover from losing a child. I am not sure. Even now, I remember walking into my house on December 14, 2012, to find my husband sobbing in front of the TV, watching as the news of Newtown emerged. We do not live in Connecticut, we knew no one involved, yet as parents ourselves we were shaken to our core and shared in their unimaginable pain.

Adam Lanza's actions revolt us. His father is so horrified by Adam's actions that he told Andrew Solomon he wished his son Adam had never been born. I cannot imagine that pain. But Peter Lanza's grief is different. It is unsanctioned grief. Unlike most mourners, Peter Lanza does not have the embrace and support of the wider community to love him and to walk with him in his grief. This is what makes unsanctioned grief the loneliest and most isolated place in which to grieve.

For Peter Lanza, unsanctioned grief must be complicated and layered. He grieves for his lost child, lost in so many ways and now in death. He grieves for the victims and their families. He grieves for a community and a country grappling with how to keep their kids safe from people like Adam Lanza, and he grieves for the radical and painful changes in his own life. Even those who wonder if Peter Lanza has some culpability by virtue of how he raised Adam must realize that Peter Lanza is also a mourner.

Peter Lanza may be an extreme case of unsanctioned grief, but he is hardly alone: a closeted gay man whose partner dies, a mistress whose lover dies—these are also unsanctioned losses. How can they possibly seek the solace of others without revealing their secret relationship? It places them in a double bind: they can't receive the support of the community without revealing their relationship, and if they reveal their relationship, they fear they will be stigmatized rather than supported.

Rape, abortion, domestic violence—each is cloaked in secrecy, and each has its own particular challenges. Consider a Catholic woman lamenting her abortion. Where does she go? With whom does she speak? For many, abortion broaches the question of an unforgivable sin. Even assisting a woman to receive an abortion is grounds for excommunication within the Catholic Church. Project Rachel is a national program through the Catholic Church to help break the silence. Women who seek forgiveness and lament having chosen abortion have somewhere to go and people to talk to who understand their particular grief.

Unsanctioned grief presents a unique set of challenges. Mourners feel isolated and alone. They have no access to traditional forms of grief support. Imagine Peter Lanza walking into a grief support group in Connecticut. It's unthinkable. Unsanctioned grief mourners do not have what many mourners need most: the ability to share their grief story with others freely.

Habit of resilience

SEEK FORGIVENESS

When we think of forgiveness, often our first thoughts go to others who have knowingly or unwittingly hurt us. Perhaps we even consider those we've hurt. Unsanctioned grief may present a different conundrum. How do we forgive ourselves?

Forgiving ourselves is hard work. Perhaps we believe we have done something that has removed us beyond the bounds of God's forgiveness. We may feel exiled, beyond the reach of grace. Unsanctioned grief and our own sense that we are outside the bounds of forgiveness deepen our isolation. But we are made to live in community and in connection with others. When there is a rupture in our connection with others, we must find a way to repair the breach.

REFLECTION

What do you need to forgive? To whom can you tell your story? Who will hear your truth? Who will hold all the rawness and pain in your sacred story?

Can you fearlessly consider the damage your actions may have caused another? What might you do to repair the damage?

Does your faith tradition have a practice of reconciliation? How will you reconcile with God and your community?

Moving through grief to grace

✕ 18 ✕

CHOOSING RESILIENCE AS VETERANS AND EVERYDAY PILGRIMS

Stand by the roads and look, and ask for the ancient paths,
where the good way is, and walk in it, and find rest for your souls.
JEREMIAH 6:16

Our returning military veterans have a tough road to travel. They often return to communities who cannot fathom what the veteran has seen or done and cannot fully appreciate the emotional complexity of vets fearing for their lives and living—when so many of their buddies died. Zara Renander, author and founder of Turning Point Consultants, whom we met in the Prologue, has significant experience helping veterans deal with the spiritual wounds that need healing. Renander offered this:

> As we welcome home our service men and women from what are often multiple deployments in war zones, they frequently carry with them deep grief and a sense of moral injury. Moral injury occurs when we are required to act in a way that damages our conscience and our own deep sense of who we are at our heart's core. The occasions during war for moral injury are multitudinous. For example: if a soldier

shoots at a car of a suspected enemy to find later that the car contains children as well who have all died in the wreckage, moral injury is likely to occur. The variations on this example are essentially unlimited.

Today we live in a world where the majority of young people have no religious background. They do not have a sacred story that tells them that they can never go so far from God's grace that forgiveness is impossible. When their consciences carry this impossible burden, they have nowhere to turn and seem trapped in a dark tunnel of self-incrimination and shame. Talk therapy, while important, is not always enough to release the pain and grief allowing them to move to a new place in their lives. This is where the labyrinth and pilgrimage become important embodied rituals, allowing participants to ritually release pain and the sense of being stuck in grief, to accept blessing and to move into new life and purpose.[1]

Renander incorporates both pilgrimage and the labyrinth in her work with veterans and others. A pilgrimage is a journey, usually long, and the destination is normally to a sacred site. One of the most common pilgrimages for Christians is the Way of St. James, also known as *El Camino de Santiago*. The pilgrimage can take weeks or months, and it has multiple routes traversing northwestern Spain to the Cathedral of Santiago de Compostela in Galicia.

The most common route for the Camino begins in the French

---

1   Zara Renander, personal letter.

Pyrenees. This 500-mile route typically takes about thirty-five days. The physical act of walking a hot and dusty path day after day defines this incarnational spiritual work. You get up, put on your boots, and follow the yellow signs for "the way." Walk ten to fifteen miles, and find a hostel. Eat, sleep. Repeat.

The act of walking day after day strips us to our bare essentials. We cannot possibly carry all we will need for the journey, nor can we anticipate what might be most needed or wanted in our backpack. Do we stow a raincoat only to hike thirty-five days in dry heat? Do we bring an extra pair of running shoes "just in case"?

Serendipity plays a large part in the spiritual work of the pilgrim. Much of the interior work is done as we place one foot in front of the other, moment after moment and day after day. Thoughts we'd love to avoid are unavoidable and ideas we hoped to meditate on can float off like wispy clouds. Other pilgrims will cross our path, unexpected companions on our journey who spark ideas, conversations, and companionship.

Pilgrims often discover things they already knew at some level. Sometimes the discovery is an epiphany, a flash of clarity when we see old things in a new light. Sometimes they rediscover an old truth, something known but forgotten. Sometimes pilgrims learn something new and come face to face with one of their deep fears. Pilgrims discover plenty along the way.

1.   We are not in control. Not of the weather. Not of the crowds in the hostels. Not of whether we get killer blisters with our new boots. In our day-to-day life, we may have created the illusion that we are in control, but the veil of this illusion often lifts on a pilgrimage.

2.   We are profoundly dependent on the kindness and mercy of strangers. A shared orange is sweeter when it is an unexpected offering miles from our next stop. Stopping to help bandage a fellow traveler's blisters will make the difference of whether he finishes the trip or suffers in agony. The generosity of others radiates warmth and good humor in our lives. If we can embody this insight, we realize that our own generosity and welcome radiate hope into others' lives as well. What we say and offer—our kindness and generosity—to others, it makes all the difference.

3.   Walking helps us view our lives from a new perspective. When we walk it through rather than talk it through or think it through, our insights are different. Walking reveals to us what thinking and talking alone have not.

4.   Remember #1? We aren't in control. We wrestle with what bubbles up, but we don't control what bubbles up. What pricks in our consciousness over 500 miles step by step might surprise us. Many pilgrims return home before they realize what new insights the Camino imprinted on their hearts.

5.   It really is about the journey, not the destination. Pilgrims headed for the Cathedral of Santiago de Compostela surely start with the intention of kneeling in front of the statue of St. James, placing their hand on the worn bronze of the statue, and offering their prayer of thanksgiving. But ultimately, our thanksgiving is not offered for the chance to kneel at the statue;

we could have flown in directly, missed 500 miles of walking, and saved a lot of sweat and blisters. Our gratitude is for the journey itself and our new insight and awareness.

6.   When we abandon the notion that we have to rely entirely on ourselves, we can lighten up. Pilgrims invariably end their journeys with a much lighter pack than they started with. They have shared the contents of their packs, shed unnecessary items, and learned that even in the company of strangers, we need less than we think we do.

Not all of us can afford the time or expense of a month-long pilgrimage. For those wanting a pilgrimage experience closer to home, consider a labyrinth. A labyrinth, according to Zara Renander, who is not only a pilgrimage leader but also the author of *Labyrinths: Journeys of Healing, Stories of Grace*, "is a sacred journey, made within the confines of a circle… Some dismiss the idea of the labyrinth as a pilgrimage, thinking that the actual distance is too short to make the claim. However, the walk is never about the geographic distance… it is [about] the spiritual depths that are plumbed."[2]

Renander reminds us that the labyrinth is more than a symbolic pilgrimage; it is a powerful spiritual tool. At first glance, a labyrinth might look like a maze. It is, in fact, the antithesis of a maze. A maze is designed to trick you, to send you down false paths, dead ends, and circles. A labyrinth does the opposite. Simply putting one foot

---

2   Zara Renander, *Labyrinths: Journeys of Healing, Stories of Grace* (Sarasota, FL: Bardolf & Co., 2011), pp. 12, 23.

in front of the other with the confidence that we need only follow the path to reach the center frees our mind to allow other, deeper thoughts to emerge.

There are many ways and reasons to walk the labyrinth. Some walk to become more aware of the questions that are bubbling up in their subconscious. As they walk, they simply give attention to whatever thoughts surface. Others begin their labyrinth walks with more intentionality, perhaps journaling before their walk so that they might have a specific focus for their walk. Some walk to help process old wounds and find the labyrinth to be a healing path.

Habit of resilience

BE A PILGRIM

Many pilgrims begin their pilgrimage with a stone from home to place on the path as they walk. In Renander's work, the stone represents something that needs healing and forgiveness that continues to weigh the pilgrim down.

The practice of carrying a stone on pilgrimage is also a powerful meditation when walking the labyrinth. Choose a stone of significant heft, something that will literally weigh you down. As you carry the stone, meditate on what it is that you carry in your heart that also weighs you down. How do you benefit from carrying this burden? What does it cost you to continue to carry this burden? As you carry the stone, remember you have the power to put the stone down and leave the burden behind when you choose.

As you carry this weight, remember that you can't rewrite this past chapter in your life. You can't change the past. All the "if onlys" bouncing around in your head are not helpful; no amount of wishful thinking will create an alternative past. You can only choose how to move on now.

Feel the true burden of this weight. Ponder the full weight of this burden. What do you gain from hanging onto this weight? What would it feel like to put this weight down, to forgive yourself, and to move on?

When you feel ready, place the stone along the path. Leave this stone for the divine to carry on. This place is your holy ground, the place you chose to let the past simply be the past.

REFLECTION

What rock are you carrying? What is it costing you to continue to carry this rock? What would it take to forgive yourself, and to set the rock down?

Is there anything in your life you feel is truly unforgivable? Whom might you talk to about this?

❄ 19 ❄

FEED THE WOLF
OF COMPASSION

*"A man dies when he refuses to stand up for that which is right.
A man dies when he refuses to stand up for justice. A man dies
when he refuses to take a stand for that which is true."*

MARTIN LUTHER KING JR.[3]

Remember the biblical story of Joseph, Jacob's son, who received a multicolored coat from his father? Joseph was Jacob's eleventh son and Rachel's firstborn. Rachel was Jacob's true love. Laban, her father, had tricked Jacob into marrying Rachel's older sister Leah; Jacob indentured himself for an additional seven years to win Rachel as his second wife. Until she gave birth, Rachel was thought to be barren, so Joseph's arrival was a joyful surprise, and his father doted on him.

Joseph lived in a blended family drama of biblical proportions; he had ten half-brothers, the sons of Leah, one younger brother, Benjamin, and one half-sister. Joseph was cosseted and educated by

---

3   Selma, AL sermon by Martin Luther King, Jr. on March 8, 1965, quoted in Frederick W. Mayer, *Narrative Politics: Stories and Collective Action* (New York: Oxford University Press, 2014), p. 133.

his father, Jacob, while his brothers tended farm. Not surprisingly, his brothers were venomously jealous of Joseph.

By all accounts, Joseph was arrogant and conceited. He also lacked much self-awareness. This combination was nearly lethal for Joseph. Yet he blithely shared his dreams with his family, either unaware or unconcerned as to how they might be received. In one dream, he and his brothers gather sheaves of grain. His brothers' sheaves encircle Joseph's bundle and begin bowing down to it. His second dream was no less infuriating to his brothers. In this dream, his eleven brothers are represented as stars, his father as the sun, and his mother as the moon. This time, the stars, the sun, and the moon bowed down to Joseph. Imagine how well this went over with his ten older half-brothers.

Joseph was dubbed the dreamer; I'd guess his brothers had a few other choice names for him as well. One day when his brothers saw Joseph coming from a distance, they connived to kill him by lowering him into a well. Then, they reconsidered. Why not sell him as a slave instead to the Egyptian caravans passing through? They got rid of him and made a profit, too.

Life went on in Jacob's household. Jacob was told that Joseph was killed by wild beasts and given his bloody clothes as evidence. Meanwhile, Joseph had his own adventures in Egypt: hard work, deception, temptation, prison, malice, and redemption. In the end, Joseph interprets a few dreams for the Pharaoh and becomes second in command. Not a bad gig for a kid sold to slave traders by his brothers.

Joseph correctly interprets the Pharaoh's dream that Egypt and the surrounding area will have seven years of abundance, followed by seven years of famine. Joseph sets up a rationing program to save a percentage of the grain each year in the prosperous years so they might survive the famine. All is well in Egypt, thanks to Joseph's ability to interpret dreams and his land management program.

Meanwhile, Jacob's household comes perilously close to starvation. Knowing Egypt has grain to trade, Jacob sends his sons to Egypt for food. When they arrive with silver in hand for trade, whom should they encounter but Joseph?—whom they do not recognize.

You've got to love the story at this point. Joseph's dream has come true—and I suspect in more ways than one. His old dream about the grain sheaves bowing down before him has been fulfilled. Can't you imagine Joseph dreaming of sweet revenge for his deceitful older brothers? Joseph proves himself fully human as he toys with revenge, throwing one brother in prison for a supposed theft, and watching the others squirm. With the tables turned, Joseph now holds all the power, and like his brothers, he uses his power in an abusive and corrupt way, at least briefly.

The Native American tradition has a story of the two wolves. One wolf is compassionate, forgiving, and merciful; the other is vengeful and full of hate and bitterness. According to the story, each wolf lives inside of us, and each battles for dominance. Ultimately, which wolf will grow stronger and dominate the other? The wolf you feed.

When Joseph encounters his brothers again, he has the power to either save their lives or imprison them. It is a turning point; he can either choose to feed the wolf of sweet revenge, or feed the wolf of forgiveness. Ultimately, he chooses forgiveness, revealing himself to his brothers and saying, "You meant this to me for evil, but God meant it to me for good." In Joseph's moment of true clarity, he realizes that God can redeem anything.

When we are faced with a tragic loss, we too must make a choice. Will we feed the wolf of bitterness and spend our life ranting about how we were grievously wronged, or will we feed the wolf of compassion and healing, allowing God to redeem the tragedy so that it might bear the fruit of great blessing for others?

In 1985, when she was a senior in college with only six weeks to graduation, Al and Mary Kluesner's daughter Amy suicided. Al and Mary had no hint that Amy was depressed. As Al and Mary began the long process of unraveling the last months of Amy's depression, they discovered she had stopped attending classes. She had also disengaged with her friends and classmates. In hindsight, her parents believed she had demonstrated clear signs of depression. But Amy was an adult, and colleges are vigilant about their students' privacy. No one contacted the Kluesners with their concerns about Amy until it was too late.

Mental health is a tricky conundrum. We want to protect the privacy of others, yet we need to know how and when to intervene. Amy's parents believe Amy's death resulted from untreated depression. Sadly, clinically depressed people are often the last to request help; their depressions bog them down and cloud their thinking, making it difficult to take the initiative to advocate for themselves. Mary and Al would have gladly advocated for Amy, but they never got the chance.

Amy's story and legacy do not stop there. Al and Mary continued to educate themselves about suicide. They met with other survivors of suicide, parents like themselves who had been blindsided by their sons' and daughters' suicides. Collectively they took the words of Madeleine L'Engle to heart. "We have to be braver than we think we can be, because God is constantly calling us to be more than we are."[4]

---

4   Madeleine L'Engle, *Walking on Water: Reflections on Faith and Art* (New York: North Point Press, 1995), p. 67.

These couples, all parents who had children die by suicide, founded S.A.V.E., Suicide Awareness Voices of Education. "The mission of SAVE is to prevent suicide through public awareness and education, reduce stigma and serve as a resource to those touched by suicide." (www.SAVE.org)

For decades, SAVE has been at the national forefront of educating others that suicide is a public health issue. For too long we have treated the brain and mental illness like a character flaw rather than an illness. We have stigmatized the illness rather than recognizing it as a brain sickness that needs treatment. We forget that the brain, like every other organ, can become ill. When the brain gets sick with depressive brain illness, it needs treatment just like any other organ in our body.

I would like to end the story there, but sadly, that is not the end of the story for Al and Mary. In 1997, their son Michael suicided. Michael's mental illness was intractable, defying the best treatment options available. Depressive illnesses are not unlike many cancers; sometimes, our very best treatment options are not enough. Yet even after Michael's death, Al and Mary continued to work so that some-day better treatments and awareness of suicide might save others.

Habit of resilience

CHOOSE COMPASSION OVER BITTERNESS

There is a saying in grief support: Get better or get bitter. Like the biblical Joseph, we have a choice to make, to lash out in spite and hate, or to choose love and hope as our legacy. Most of the turning points in our lives are not as dramatic as Joseph's, yet they help to clarify our choice to channel our energy in positive or negative ways. I imagine that many nights Al and Mary Kleusner were inconsolable, heart-broken, and enraged at the many ways the system had failed Amy. It was an epic failure, and it cost Amy her life. Yet in the end, they have chosen love and hope.

REFLECTION

Sometimes early in our grief process we are too overwhelmed to consider what legacy might emerge to honor our loved one. Legacies can evolve in unexpected ways. We may be surprised to discover our grief work has become a blessing to others. Can you think of some examples where tragedy has been transformed to blessing for others?

When we tap into our best self, we more easily choose to feed the wolf of compassion. But sometimes we react before we reflect. What helps you to stop to be more compassionate and generous when you are tempted to feed the wolf of bitterness?

❧ 20 ❧

CHOOSING RESILIENCE
ONE SMALL STEP AT A TIME

Patience is not waiting passively until someone else does something.
Patience asks us to live the moment to the fullest, to be completely present
to the moment, to taste the here and now, to be where we are…
Be patient and trust that the treasure you are looking for is hidden
in the ground on which you stand. HENRI NOUWEN[5]

Remember Newton's First Law of Motion? A body in motion stays in motion; a body at rest stays at rest. It turns out that physics has plenty to do with how we kick-start our grief process. To *get* going is monumentally more difficult than to *keep* going. Transitioning from a full stop to a new life is hard work. Going out alone can shake your world if you've always done this as a couple. Imagine the initiative needed. Sometimes in grief, we have to force ourselves to do something, even if it is small. Doing a little often starts with noticing. The late Wangari Maathai won the Nobel Peace Prize not because she did something staggeringly difficult. She won because she noticed something troubling

---

5   Henri Nouwen, *Bread for the Journey: A Daybook of Wisdom and Faith*
(New York: HarperCollins, 1997), p. 1

forty years ago and she did one small thing to help. In a 2006 commencement speech at Connecticut College, she said, "I noticed the
rivers became brown during the rainy season."

Brown rivers during rainy season may mean little to you and me,
but in Kenya, muddy water means undrinkable water.

Maathai surmised that the change had to do with how land in
Kenya was being used and cultivated.

Great swaths of scrubby brush land were being cleared for tea and
coffee plantations. On a smaller scale, villagers cut down trees for
firewood. The combination of these forces meant there was less vege-
tation to hold the soil. During Kenya's rainy season, erosion increased
dramatically. The rain washed away precious topsoil and muddied
drinking water. Undrinkable water was only part of the problem. As
the topsoil eroded, the land became less fertile.

Before Maathai revealed what she did about Kenya's muddy rivers
she shared a South American folk tale about a hummingbird and a
wildfire.

> A forest fire was blazing out of control and all the animals
> fled to safety and watched from a distance. The humming-
> bird flew to a small stream, took a drop of water in its beak
> and flew back over the fire to drop the precious water. The
> hummingbird did this again and again and again. The other
> animals mocked the little bird. The bird's efforts seemed
> futile; such an enormous fire, such a little bird. Undeterred,
> the bird responded. "I'm doing the best I can."[6]

6   Maathai, Wangari, "88th Connecticut College Commencement Address"
(2006). Commencement Addresses. Paper 8. http://digitalcommons.conncoll.
edu/commence/8

Maathai then shared her Nobel-Prize-winning solution. She planted a tree. Trees, she reasoned, held the key to clean water. Collectively, many trees would once again hold the soil. The rivers would become clearer and the water more drinkable. Maathai convinced other women that they, too, should plant a tree. With one tree, the Green Belt Movement was born in Kenya.

Maathai's solution was simple and elegant. Each person did one small thing. And this small act of planting a tree changed their lives and their community for good.

Habit of resilience

DO SOMETHING, EVEN IF IT IS SMALL

When a loved one dies, our world seems to stop. Some days the simplest daily tasks seem to take more energy than we have. Even the smallest steps forward can feel monumentally difficult. But taking small steps are important because they get us moving again.

If you feel stuck in your grief, the challenge in the epilogue will help you get going again. I encourage you to take that challenge.

REFLECTION

As you think back on your grief, what are the small things you did—or could do now—to propel yourself back into living a fuller life?

Loneliness and aloneness are related but different aspects of grief. Our aloneness may make us feel awkward about going to a movie or out to dinner solo. Has your aloneness kept you from doing something you'd like to do? What small step might you make to move forward?

Epilogue

PRACTICING GRATITUDE AS A HABIT OF RESILIENCE

Give thanks in all circumstances.

1 THESSALONIANS 5:18

Resilience is like a muscle. The more we use it, the stronger we get. There are plenty of things we can do to enhance our resilience: eat a balanced diet of nutritious food, get enough sleep, stay connected with friends and family, avoid abusing drugs and alcohol, and exercise. We can also adopt a stance of gratitude. Expressing gratitude transforms our outlook and worldview for the better. Gratitude transforms us—body, mind, and spirit.

21-day gratitude challenge

Let's talk about the happiness myth. We have this common belief that happiness is pegged to our external environment. If everything is great in our world, our families are healthy, our children above average, and we have a great job—then we will be happy. When something is amiss, we've lost a loved one, and we're grieving—naturally we are justifiably miserable.

But it's not as simple as this. Our happiness is not determined primarily by external circumstances; it is linked to our mindset. It turns out that only a tiny fraction of our happiness is determined by our external environment. Happiness is overwhelmingly determined by our mindset. Our reality doesn't shape our worldview—the way we look at our world shapes our reality.

If this is true, if the way in which we view the world is the largest predictor of how we feel, how can we change our view? How do we move beyond merely coping to a place of healing and hope? How do we build resilience in a time of stress and loss?

Practicing gratitude prepares us to be resilient. Gratitude improves the way we feel, and when we feel better, we have a greater capacity to stretch ourselves. Here are five simple practices, a spiritual perspective on structured activities presented by Shawn Achor in his TED Talk, "The Happiness Advantage."[1]

BLESSINGS AND GRATITUDE. Remember to count your blessings. Each day write down *new* things that are blessings in your life. This will help you retrain your mind to scan for the blessings in your life. Because you are looking for and expecting blessings, you will notice them more easily.

JOURNALING JOY. Write a brief journal entry of something that brought you joy. The event can come from any time in your life and can

---

1 Shawn Achor, "The Happiness Advantage," 6/30/11. Found 10/4/2015 at https://www.youtube.com/watch?v=GXy__kBVq1M

be a very small event. Your write-up can be short, maybe a paragraph. By writing about these past blessings, you relive the positive emotions.

EXERCISE. Thirty minutes of moderate exercise three times a week is a proven antidepressant. Doctors prescribe exercise for a host of ailments: heart disease, diabetes, and depression, among others. Let's throw grief on the list—it helps with that too. Physical activity is inversely related to depression, which means that ramping up your body's aerobic exercise is likely to damp down depressed feelings. Even a modest plan of thirty minutes three times a week can significantly improve how you feel.

MEDITATE OR PRAY. Stop each day for at least five minutes to meditate or pray. Prayer helps us realign our spirit with the sacred. Silence your phone, turn off the TV, and find quiet space to center yourself in prayer each day.

RANDOM ACTS OF KINDNESS. We can't spread the love of a random act of kindness without being fully present in the moment. My husband noticed a young mother coming up a few cents short while trying to buy three caramels for her young children. My husband slipped a few coins on the counter. It was a small gesture, but it demanded that he be present to the opportunity and notice the needs of others. Being present helps us take the microscope off our troubles so we can consider the needs of others. It doesn't minimize our difficulties. It simply shifts our perspective.

The following pages are designed for you to take the 21-day Habits of Resilience challenge. Want more ideas for developing resilience? Visit us at www.HabitsofResilience.com. May it be a blessing.

21-DAY CHALLENGE
A heart of gratitude

day 1 Date: _____

GRATITUDE

1) _____

2) _____

3) _____

RANDOM ACT OF KINDNESS

Today I... _____

_____

_____

PRAYER/MEDITATION

Start time: _____

End time: _____

EXERCISE

What: _____

How long: _____

JOURNAL: *An event from the past that brought you joy or happiness*

_____

_____

_____

_____

_____

_____

_____

_____

_____

_____

21-DAY CHALLENGE
A heart of gratitude

day 2 Date: _____

GRATITUDE

1) _____

2) _____

3) _____

RANDOM ACT OF KINDNESS

Today I... _____

_____

_____

PRAYER/MEDITATION

Start time: _____

End time: _____

EXERCISE

What: _____

How long: _____

JOURNAL: *An event from the past that brought you joy or happiness*

_____

_____

_____

_____

_____

_____

_____

_____

_____

_____

A heart of gratitude

day 3 Date: _____

GRATITUDE

1) _____

2) _____

3) _____

RANDOM ACT OF KINDNESS

Today I... _____

_____

_____

PRAYER/MEDITATION

Start time: _____

End time: _____

EXERCISE

What: _____

How long: _____

JOURNAL: *An event from the past that brought you joy or happiness*

_____

_____

_____

_____

_____

_____

_____

_____

_____

_____

21-DAY CHALLENGE
A heart of gratitude

day 4 Date: _____

GRATITUDE

1) _____

2) _____

3) _____

RANDOM ACT OF KINDNESS

Today I... _____

_____

_____

PRAYER/MEDITATION

Start time: _____

End time: _____

EXERCISE

What: _____

How long: _____

JOURNAL: *An event from the past that brought you joy or happiness*

_____

_____

_____

_____

_____

_____

_____

_____

_____

_____

21-DAY CHALLENGE
A heart of gratitude

day 5 Date: _____

GRATITUDE

1) _____

2) _____

3) _____

RANDOM ACT OF KINDNESS

Today I... _____

_____

_____

PRAYER/MEDITATION

Start time: _____

End time: _____

EXERCISE

What: _____

How long: _____

JOURNAL: *An event from the past that brought you joy or happiness*

_____

_____

_____

_____

_____

_____

_____

_____

_____

_____

21-DAY CHALLENGE
A heart of gratitude

day 6 Date: _____

GRATITUDE

1) _____

2) _____

3) _____

RANDOM ACT OF KINDNESS

Today I... _____

_____

_____

PRAYER/MEDITATION

Start time: _____

End time: _____

EXERCISE

What: _____

How long: _____

JOURNAL: *An event from the past that brought you joy or happiness*

_____

_____

_____

_____

_____

_____

_____

_____

_____

_____

A heart of gratitude

day 7 Date: _____

GRATITUDE

1) _____

2) _____

3) _____

RANDOM ACT OF KINDNESS

Today I... _____

_____

_____

PRAYER/MEDITATION

Start time: _____

End time: _____

EXERCISE

What: _____

How long: _____

JOURNAL: *An event from the past that brought you joy or happiness*

_____

_____

_____

_____

_____

_____

_____

_____

_____

_____

21-DAY CHALLENGE
A heart of gratitude

Date: _____

GRATITUDE

1) _____

2) _____

3) _____

RANDOM ACT OF KINDNESS

Today I... _____

_____

_____

PRAYER/MEDITATION

Start time: _____

End time: _____

EXERCISE

What: _____

How long: _____

JOURNAL: *An event from the past that brought you joy or happiness*

_____

_____

_____

_____

_____

_____

_____

_____

_____

_____

_____

21-DAY CHALLENGE
A heart of gratitude

day 9 | Date: _____

GRATITUDE

1) _____

2) _____

3) _____

RANDOM ACT OF KINDNESS

Today I... _____

_____

_____

PRAYER/MEDITATION

Start time: _____

End time: _____

EXERCISE

What: _____

How long: _____

JOURNAL: *An event from the past that brought you joy or happiness*

_____

_____

_____

_____

_____

_____

_____

_____

_____

_____

21-DAY CHALLENGE
A heart of gratitude

day 10 Date: _____

GRATITUDE

1) _____

2) _____

3) _____

RANDOM ACT OF KINDNESS

Today I... _____

_____

_____

PRAYER/MEDITATION

Start time: _____

End time: _____

EXERCISE

What: _____

How long: _____

JOURNAL: *An event from the past that brought you joy or happiness*

_____

_____

_____

_____

_____

_____

_____

_____

_____

_____

21-DAY CHALLENGE
A heart of gratitude

day 11 Date: _____

GRATITUDE	RANDOM ACT OF KINDNESS
1) _____	*Today I...* _____
2) _____	_____
3) _____	_____

PRAYER/MEDITATION	EXERCISE
Start time: _____	What: _____
End time: _____	How long: _____

JOURNAL: *An event from the past that brought you joy or happiness*

_____

_____

_____

_____

_____

_____

_____

_____

_____

21-DAY CHALLENGE
A heart of gratitude

day 12 Date: _____

GRATITUDE

1) _____

2) _____

3) _____

RANDOM ACT OF KINDNESS

Today I... _____

_____

_____

PRAYER/MEDITATION

Start time: _____

End time: _____

EXERCISE

What: _____

How long: _____

JOURNAL: *An event from the past that brought you joy or happiness*

_____

_____

_____

_____

_____

_____

_____

_____

_____

_____

21-DAY CHALLENGE
A heart of gratitude

day 13 Date: _____

GRATITUDE

1) _____

2) _____

3) _____

RANDOM ACT OF KINDNESS

Today I... _____

_____

_____

PRAYER/MEDITATION

Start time: _____

End time: _____

EXERCISE

What: _____

How long: _____

JOURNAL: *An event from the past that brought you joy or happiness*

_____

_____

_____

_____

_____

_____

_____

_____

_____

_____

21-DAY CHALLENGE
A heart of gratitude

day 14 Date: _____

GRATITUDE

1) _____

2) _____

3) _____

RANDOM ACT OF KINDNESS

Today I... _____

_____

_____

PRAYER/MEDITATION

Start time: _____

End time: _____

EXERCISE

What: _____

How long: _____

JOURNAL: *An event from the past that brought you joy or happiness*

_____

_____

_____

_____

_____

_____

_____

_____

_____

_____

21-DAY CHALLENGE
A heart of gratitude

day 15 Date: _____

GRATITUDE

1) _____

2) _____

3) _____

RANDOM ACT OF KINDNESS

Today I... _____

_____

_____

PRAYER/MEDITATION

Start time: _____

End time: _____

EXERCISE

What: _____

How long: _____

JOURNAL: *An event from the past that brought you joy or happiness*

_____

_____

_____

_____

_____

_____

_____

_____

_____

_____

21-DAY CHALLENGE
A heart of gratitude

GRATITUDE

1) _____

2) _____

3) _____

RANDOM ACT OF KINDNESS

Today I... _____

_____

_____

PRAYER/MEDITATION

Start time: _____

End time: _____

EXERCISE

What: _____

How long: _____

JOURNAL: *An event from the past that brought you joy or happiness*

_____

_____

_____

_____

_____

_____

_____

_____

_____

_____

21-DAY CHALLENGE
A heart of gratitude

GRATITUDE

1) _____

2) _____

3) _____

RANDOM ACT OF KINDNESS

Today I... _____

_____

_____

PRAYER/MEDITATION

Start time: _____

End time: _____

EXERCISE

What: _____

How long: _____

JOURNAL: *An event from the past that brought you joy or happiness*

_____

_____

_____

_____

_____

_____

_____

_____

_____

_____

21-DAY CHALLENGE
A heart of gratitude

GRATITUDE

1) _____

2) _____

3) _____

RANDOM ACT OF KINDNESS

Today I... _____

_____

_____

PRAYER/MEDITATION

Start time: _____

End time: _____

EXERCISE

What: _____

How long: _____

JOURNAL: *An event from the past that brought you joy or happiness*

_____

_____

_____

_____

_____

_____

_____

_____

_____

A heart of gratitude

day 19 Date: _____

GRATITUDE

1) _____

2) _____

3) _____

RANDOM ACT OF KINDNESS

Today I... _____

_____

_____

PRAYER/MEDITATION

Start time: _____

End time: _____

EXERCISE

What: _____

How long: _____

JOURNAL: *An event from the past that brought you joy or happiness*

_____

_____

_____

_____

_____

_____

_____

_____

_____

_____

21-DAY CHALLENGE
A heart of gratitude

Date: _____

GRATITUDE

1) _____

2) _____

3) _____

RANDOM ACT OF KINDNESS

Today I... _____

_____

_____

PRAYER/MEDITATION

Start time: _____

End time: _____

EXERCISE

What: _____

How long: _____

JOURNAL: *An event from the past that brought you joy or happiness*

_____

_____

_____

_____

_____

_____

_____

_____

_____

_____

21-DAY CHALLENGE
A heart of gratitude

Date: _____

GRATITUDE

1) _____

2) _____

3) _____

RANDOM ACT OF KINDNESS

Today I... _____

_____

_____

PRAYER/MEDITATION

Start time: _____

End time: _____

EXERCISE

What: _____

How long: _____

JOURNAL: *An event from the past that brought you joy or happiness*

_____

_____

_____

_____

_____

_____

_____

_____

_____

_____

Acknowledgments

No book encouraging gratitude would be complete without proper thanks for the many people who generously offered their time and guidance. Trish Vanni nudged this project into being over coffee. My thanks to Twenty-Third Publications for their willingness to support a book on resilience and for their editorial assistance. Years ago, Karla Wennerstrom, editor of the *Eden Prairie News*, graciously invited me to write a column in my local newspaper, and the ensuing deadlines became the genesis of many of the stories in this book moving onto the written page.

Along with reading the manuscript, Patricia and Fred Baumer suggested a structure and gave the book its cadence, and Wharton Sinkler stretched and broadened my perspective—reminding me not to believe everything I believe! Zara Renander generously offered hours of conversation on resilience and shared her experience working with veterans, including those suffering from PTSD. Readers Martha Baker, Vicky Shields, Deb Paone, Carol Smith, Micki O'Flynn, and Terry Naugle offered their wisdom and encouragement. Paula Berry started as a trusted administrative assistant and ended up a dear friend. She read and reread the book, offering fresh eyes and enthusiasm. Many grief support groups in the Twin Cities invited me to speak, allowing me to try out and adapt this work. Finally, I appreciate all the opportunities I've been given to teach and coach companion ministry and Stephen Ministry—there is no better way to learn your craft than conveying it to others. Thank you all for your invaluable contributions!

My deep thanks go to the many who shared their stories with me: the families who invited a complete stranger into a hospital room or their home, trusting me with their raw and wrenching pain. And to my husband, Steve, who has been my best example of living a resilient life, thanks is simply too small a word.